The Geometry of Hunger

Books by D. S. Halacy, Jr.

The
Geometry of Hunger

D. S. Halacy, Jr.

HARPER & ROW, PUBLISHERS

NEW YORK, EVANSTON, SAN FRANCISCO, LONDON

1817

THE GEOMETRY OF HUNGER. Copyright © 1972 by D. S. Halacy, Jr. All rights reserved. Printed in the United States of America. No part of this book may be used or reproduced in any manner whatsoever without written permission except in the case of brief quotations embodied in critical articles and reviews. For information address Harper & Row, Publishers, Inc., 49 East 33rd Street, New York, N.Y. 10016. Published simultaneously in Canada by Fitzhenry & Whiteside Limited, Toronto.

FIRST EDITION

STANDARD BOOK NUMBER: 06-011746-X

LIBRARY OF CONGRESS CATALOG CARD NUMBER: 71-156525

Designed by C. Linda Dingler

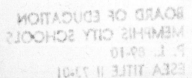

Contents

Part I.

The People Problem

> The battle to feed all of humanity is over. In the 1970's the world will undergo famines—hundreds of millions of people are going to starve to death in spite of any crash programs embarked upon now. . . .
>
> Prologue to *The Population Bomb* by Paul Ehrlich

CHAPTER 1

Doomsday, November 13

In the year 1800 the Reverend Thomas R. Malthus, who besides being a minister also had a degree in economics, pointed out that man was doomed to widespread famines because he bred faster than the food supply could be increased. In the year 1960, scientists Heinz von Foerster, Patricia M. Mora, and Lawrence W. Amiot, writing in the journal *Science*, hollowly echoed the Malthusian warnings by calculating "Doomsday" to its very calendar date. Doomsday, they announced, would occur on November 13, 2026. By that time the world would have a population of 50 billion and a population density of 10,000 per square mile of land surface!

Since that prediction, many other scientists and laymen alike have become prophets of doom. Garrett Hardin, Paul Ehrlich, George Borgstrom, and the Paddock brothers, William and Paul, are among those who warn of the coming horrors of the overproduction of people and the underproduction of food.

In an age of press-agentry and cute sloganism, the term "population explosion" tends to conjure up ludicrous visions of humanity suddenly swelling like a newly created volcano, about to erupt a lava flow of flesh all over the landscape. This is not to say that the population increase, actually only about 2 percent a year, is a joke. Compared with the increase in times past, it *has* become a literal explosion.

In all the hundreds of thousands of years of man's existence on Earth, he had achieved a population of only half a billion by A.D. 1650. But in the next 200 years he produced the second half billion. Eighty years later, in 1930, the population had again doubled, and there were 2 billion humans to be fed. The next doubling—an alarming 4 billion—will have taken place by 1975. After that, only about thirty-five years will be needed to double the population again, to 8 billion.

Robert Ripley, of "Believe It or Not" fame, once dramatized the population problem by noting that if the Chinese began to march some twelve abreast past a point, they would never all of them get by: the birthrate added new Chinese faster than they could march. One wit remarked that this was hardly a fair analogy, since reproduction could hardly take place on the march. To which Ripley replied that the Chinese were mighty clever people. Today, with the line of humans far longer, there is more to worry about than laugh at.

It has been correctly pointed out that if, 5,000 years ago, Adam and Eve had first begun to produce offspring at the rate of population increase now experienced worldwide, in the intervening years human life would have increased so that today the weight of human mass would exceed that of the earth itself! Earth would be covered with humans, not just standing shoulder to shoulder, but piled many deep. It should be obvious that such an eventuality will not take place, for a variety of reasons. However, the seriousness of the population explosion is indicated by the fact that since you began reading this chapter about 250 more humans appeared on Earth. Indeed, every second you stop to consider *that* shocking truth there are 2.5 more. Each day there is a net increase in population of nearly 200,000, and each year more than 70 million!

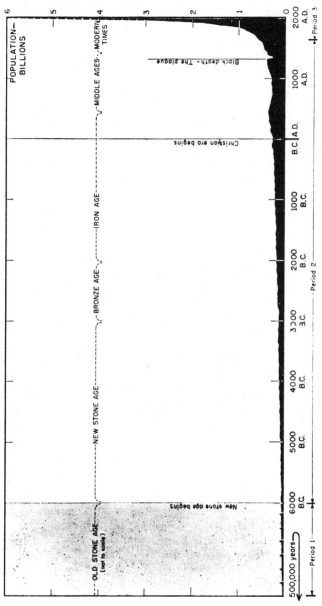

Growth of human numbers. Hundreds of thousands of years were required to reach a total of 3 billion, yet this number will be doubled in only about 35 years if current growth rates continue. The Old Stone Age is not drawn to scale; if it were it would extend about 35 feet to the left. *Reprinted with the permission of the Population Reference Bureau, Inc.*

The Best-Laid Plans of Men

Man, for all his destructiveness, is increasing his numbers appreciably. Despite homicides, the slaughter on our highways, and even the millions who have died in wars and political purges, the "explosion" continues. It is as wrong to minimize the problem—to say let's do nothing and hope it goes away—as it is to panic and suggest a benign slaughter of those less entitled to live.

For the good of our consciences, much time, effort, and money have been spent and continue to be spent on the problems of population and food. Billions of dollars have been put into researching all the facets of these problems, and there are more than most of us realize. In efforts to make a better contraceptive alone, the United States has invested tens of millions of dollars in the last several years. And we have exported millions of tons of food and thousands of experts in a variety of technical fields to help less-fortunate nations curb population growth and increase crop yields.

Many of these very problems have been created by the humanitarian instincts of people sincerely trying to do something for starving, diseased, short-lived people. Curing disease and providing more food have produced miraculous—and brutal—results, as more "have-nots" live longer lives and consequently need more food.

Part of the problem lies with nature itself. In earlier times, before the advent of efficient food production, and while wild animals and disease were rampant, life was geared to a cycle as short as fourteen or fifteen years. To preserve the human race it was necessary that its members be able to reproduce at that early age, and they are indeed physiologically able to do so. Along came medicine, sanitation, and other sciences and technologies, and now in some countries men live to be more than seventy years old on the average—five generations of reproduction. A fecund couple, dying after a long life, can leave hundreds of

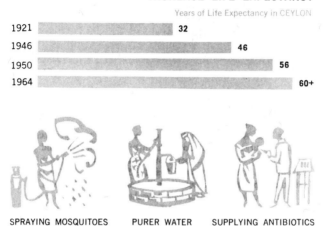

**INEXPENSIVE PUBLIC HEALTH MEASURES
INCREASE LIFE EXPECTANCY**

Years of Life Expectancy in CEYLON

1921	32
1946	46
1950	56
1964	60+

SPRAYING MOSQUITOES   PURER WATER   SUPPLYING ANTIBIOTICS

Pesticides to kill dangerous insects and thus protect mankind have
done much to prolong our lives.
Public Affairs Committee, Inc.

descendants, as an Amish couple are on record as having done.
Fewer babies die in childbirth and infancy, and adults live longer
—both ends of the population spectrum are spreading out.

Revolt of the Starving

In view of all this effort, the present situation is frustrating,
particularly to those who have labored so long and hard trying
to help. Potentially there is more danger inherent in global hunger than merely aching bellies on the one hand and frustration
on the other. Hungry people are not happy people, as Robert
McNamara pointed out when he was Secretary of Defense:

Since 1958, only one of these 27 [rich] nations has suffered a major
internal upheaval on its own territory. Among the 38 very poor na-

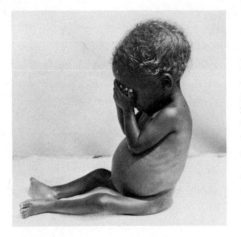

Kenya. A child sufferer from Kwashiorkor, the regional name for protein malnutrition. The condition is common in areas where diets are high in starchy foods and low in protein, and can be cured by protein-rich foods or by skim milk.
Courtesy of the Government of Kenya, issued by FAO

tions—those with a per capita income of under $100 a year—not less that 32 have suffered significant conflicts. Indeed, they have suffered an average of two major outbreaks of violence per country in the 8-year period. This is a great deal of conflict . . .

In its issue of September 1965, the *Bulletin of the Atomic Scientists* editorially embellished that idea:

The masses of people in the villages have submitted passively and quietly to starvation, with only passing notice from the West. Now, however, there is a new group of people to be reckoned with— those who have migrated to the cities and work in the new industries. They have had a taste of western living; their income, though low by our standards, has brought them more food and a higher standard of living than they ever dreamed of in their villages. These city workers will not passively submit to hunger and privation. The food rioters of India seen in the newsreels were not gaunt and emaciated; they were well-muscled, vigorous, and determined. With only a part of the population in this category a government might be forced to want to take food by force rather than submit to widespread famine.

Fertility Cult

There are hundreds of millions going hungry, and—according to some estimates—as many as 10,000 dying of starvation daily.

The problem is ironically complicated by such paradoxes as a shortage of labor in some areas of the United States, the wasting of food by many nations, the "ploughing under" and "land bank" approach to limit production of many crops, unsalable surpluses, and the apparent refusal of those on starvation diets to adapt to different kinds of foods, even when those foods are more nourishing than the traditional diet.

The push for legal abortion has reached hysterical proportions, with the Sierra Club and a number of other conservation groups clamoring against people pollution. The Hawaiian legislature in 1970 introduced a bill calling for compulsory sterilization by hospital doctors when a woman delivers her second child! The initials ZPG have assumed almost mystical significance for many people, with their goal of "Zero Population Growth" to be reached no matter what drastic steps must be taken. Some advocate onerous taxes on large families, with compensating tax breaks for those who produce no offspring, and homosexuality has been suggested by others as an answer to overpopulation. Still others suggest dosing the municipal water supply—or the atmosphere —with a contraceptive, so that a neutralizing chemical would have to be taken to effect fertilization and conception!

As we have already mentioned, our country, and other "developed" nations as well, have invested billions of dollars in helping "have-nots," providing them with food plus the know-how for increasing food production and curbing their population; indeed, some of the harder-nosed have suggested making foreign aid contingent on acceptance by the recipient nations of birth control on an enforced basis. Millions of dollars have been spent in developing and inserting IUDs, intrauterine devices designed to prevent conception. Vasectomies have been subsidized in India, with bonuses paid to men willing to undergo the operation (and with additional payment to "bounty hunters," who steer Indian males to the surgeon's knife). Results have been minimal, with populations continuing to climb and hostility also increasing as a result of such "coercion."

Population control is obviously vital. But it is not the instant cure-all that many believe it to be. If *no* more children were to be born, starting now, overcrowding would persist for many years. So would the shortage of food for many. Furthermore, societies in many backward countries are built on large families—it takes many hands to work small farms and tend animals to produce food enough for all. Many parents in such societies have children, not just because of carelessness or a love for children, but out of economic necessity. Only when there is abundance without the need for so much work by so many will such people curb their productivity.

Escape Is Difficult

In the space age it is not surprising that some suggest that man may be forced to flee in some numbers to the moon, and perhaps even to Mars, for *Lebensraum,* or to find farmland sufficient for his increasing needs. The idea is more romantic than practicable; few humans could afford rocket passage, and the success of such colonies is highly questionable. To equate the moon with the New World of Columbus's time makes better science fiction than ecological sense.

The increased production of food is an obvious requirement. With more mouths to feed there must also be more food, unless increasing millions are to go hungry. Here, however, is an area of conflicting reports and opinions. Several years ago, in the face of a "world food crisis," American farmers were urged to produce more food—and did so. In fact, they produced so prodigiously that much of their output became surplus, and the program was cut back.

Another strange food fact is that instead of land being added to cultivation in the United States, land is constantly being taken out. Orchards cut up into building lots and farms displaced by the encroaching urban octopus are familiar sights. A cartoon presented this phenomenon succinctly, with a panicky cowboy racing into camp crying a warning: "The houses are coming!" Elsewhere in the world, however, there *is* a shortage of land for farming. And there are other factors at work, often religious and superstitious in nature. For example, India is often castigated for maintaining the religious aura over its cows, thus depriving the populace not only of animal flesh but all the tons of vegetation it takes to produce this walking hamburger. In fairness, there are certain mitigating factors, which we will take up in detail later.

Some nutritionists take issue with the argument against producing meat instead of eating plants, saying that while it is indeed an "inefficient" process, it does produce better protein and other needed nutrients than can vegetation. But what of all the animal pets supported in various parts of the world, cats and dogs, horses, zoo animals, and so on? Here is a "biomass," completely unproductive as food, except in the rare instances when a laggard racehorse might end up in a can of dogfood.

The Doomsayers

Dr. Paul Ehrlich and many others claim that the battle is already lost, that we will not be able to produce enough food. As recently as 1966 there was crop failure in Asia on a colossal scale, after decades of technical assistance from American and other agricultural experts. To open up new lands requires billions of dollars in outlay for irrigation, clearing, fertilizing, and so on. And pesticides and pollution are charged with disrupting the ecology, perhaps irreversibly in some cases.

Ecologist Dr. Wayne H. Davis of the University of Kentucky calls any attempts to keep pace with population growth by producing more food total nonsense. He lumps George Borgstrom, Senator George McGovern, Orville Freeman, Lester Brown, and others as "food production boys" who are ecologically naïve. Here are excerpts from remarks by Davis in a speech to magazine editors in Louisville, Kentucky, in May 1970.

They say the population of the world will double in the next 35 years. Don't believe it; the population at the end of the century will be less than it is today. . . .

Man today is comparable to a culture of microbes enclosed in a test tube. Their numbers grow until food becomes scarce. Now the food production boys tell us that our problem is to supply more food. So we add more food and the population grows a little more until toxic waste products of their metabolism destroy the entire culture.

Man is the microbe and spaceship earth is the test tube. We have been adding food mixed with modern medicine, which has cut death rates in half and halved them again within the past 30 years in many parts of the world without concurrent reductions in birth rates. Finally we have about reached the end of our limit for the culture of organisms on spaceship earth.

So for you activists who like to see change this is a very exciting time to be alive. You won't have to sit around very long waiting for things to happen. There will be really drastic changes in this country and around the world during this decade as man approaches a desperate fight for survival. We are now awfully close to the time when the law of the jungle takes over, and within 10 years everybody who has survived will be well aware of what our real problems are.

Two Problems

The food-population problem, while it combines to produce starvation and human misery, is really several problems, each of which must be treated separately for the present. Food production is the number-one problem from a practical standpoint. The ultimate source of food—presently the energy in the sunlight that blesses us in so many other ways—is a starting place. How much of that energy can we capture through the magic of photosynthesis and the resulting "food chains" it initiates? This is the carbohydrate-protein problem—how best to solve it for the good of all? The sea—how much of a food basket does it really represent? Opinions are divergent, from those of one nutrition authority who says we can hope at best for a doubling in catch, to the optimistic estimate of sufficient protein for 30 billion humans from the bountiful sea.

Meeting of the 15th Session of the Food and Agriculture Organiza-
tion of the United Nations held in the Plenary Hall in Rome during
November, 1969.
FAO, Rome, Italy

There is the problem of human numbers itself. This entails the
reproductive process, the history of man's increasing numbers, the
prognosis for the future. How many progeny can man have, and
how should he curb that number?

Finally, and of more importance than the question of how
many humans *can* be fed, how many *should* be fed? Adam and
Eve were too few when Eden was first tainted by man's ignorance: how many billions are too many? What is the optimum
number of humans on Earth—and what are the optimum numbers
of other living things, too, for they are part of the overall
ecological system we inhabit on earth.

We have serious problems with people and food—too many of
one and too little of the other. They are agonizingly complex
problems, compounded by the false and pessimistic notions that
all of us are going to hell in a hand basket and that nobody,
America particularly, is doing anything at all about it; that some-

how all would be well if we stopped polluting the environment with pesticides; and that life was idyllic until man's science and technology ruined it.

Although we are in a worse fix than some of us realize, the situation is probably not of such catastrophic proportions as those seen by the prophets of doom. We shall begin our investigation of the population-food crunch with a look at the people explosion itself, then go on to the other aspects, including birth control, food production, pollution, and finally the consideration of optimum numbers for our human population.

Woe unto them that join house to house, that lay field
to field, till there be no place, that they may be placed
alone in the midst of the earth!

Isaiah 5:8

CHAPTER 2

The Growing Numbers

It's a common saying that the big trouble in the world is people. Without people we'd have no population explosion, of
course. So the first point to take up is population. There must
have been a time when there were *no* people—how did we get
ourselves confronted by the jackpot that now threatens? Apparently it was a long, slow process.

Since the time of the creation of man, population has surely
increased. The Biblical injunction to increase and multiply has
been amply heeded, for man has a powerful, built-in urge to
propagate the race. Procreation is a natural instinct, and for ages
man's population was controlled by natural factors alone, un-
affected by agriculture, civilization, science, or technology. Then
came these human discoveries and developments that superseded
or circumvented natural increase. That's when the trouble started.

If we had increased from one couple as fast as we did from
1900 to 1950, a mere twenty-four centuries would account for
all of today's population. This would obviously place even Bishop
Usher's date of Creation far too long ago, and most churchmen
today agree that the year 4004 B.C. was far too literal an interpre-
tation of Bible chronology. In fact, scientific estimates of the be-

ginning of human life range from about 700,000 years ago to more than 2 million years ago.

Since there were no census takers quizzing the cavemen, demographers have had to do a certain amount of detective work to arrive at rates of population growth. Accepting estimates of population at the earliest date they are available, it is then a matter of backtracking to the point when men first appeared. The increase from the first two humans to the estimated 25 million living on Earth at the time of Christ figures out to a population growth of only 1 percent per 500 years, or a doubling in about each 37,000 years, an increase slow enough to gladden the hearts of advocates for Zero Population Growth. Assuming that more than two humans touched off the population explosion—a theory that also has difficulties, it has been pointed out—the rate of growth would be even slower.

Some demographers have made much finer breakdowns of population in prehistoric times, basing their work not only on compound-interest tables read backward but also on the findings of bones, tools, and other indicators of the presence of early humans. For example, Edward S. Deevey, Jr., writing in *Scientific American*, September 1960, has estimated that 1 million years ago there were already about 125,000 humans, centered in Africa. There was only one man per 250 square kilometers, a density that would give Rhode Island a population of about 8 instead of the 860,000 it has today.

While most population curves show a slow and steady rise from the beginning of humankind until the present explosive upshooting of the curve, it is probably more accurate to display three separate curves, or "explosions," on the population-increase chart: (1) toolmaking, (2) agriculture, and (3) science-industry.

According to Deevey, there were still only about one million inhabitants of Earth 300,000 years ago. In 700,000 years the population had increased eightfold, but by expanding into new lands man had held his population density to approximately a threefold increase, or about 3 people per 250 square kilometers.

The "Toolmaking" Explosion

Early man is thought to have eaten fruits and nuts, some plants, insects, and some small animals. He was handicapped in his diet of meat by his relative helplessness compared with wild animals. Toolmaking and the harnessing of fire seem to have sparked the first population explosion, although it is doubtful that any Stone Age people noticed it as such. With tools man could now reach fruits and nuts once beyond him, and with weapons he could kill game not available to bare hands. Fire made more foods edible and also permitted the keeping of food for longer periods of time. As a result of this new wealth of food, population soared to about 5.3 million 10,000 years ago. This represented a fortyfold increase from the 1,000,000 years ago that Deevey used as his base. Yet in all the continents of the globe there still existed only one-fortieth as many people as now populate the United States alone. Ten thousand years ago there was roughly one person for each ten square miles of land surface, a very sparse settlement. This was about the extent of life support that nature provided for a hunting and gathering society. If no more cultural innovations had taken place, population might have remained relatively stable after the initial explosion.

According to Deevey, late Pleistocene man was about what would be expected in the natural scheme of things: "scarcer than the horse, but more plentiful than the elephant." According to some writers, this delightful high-protein state of affairs was deemed to be short-lived; it carried with it the seeds of its own destruction. To quote A. D. Hope:

> No hunter of the Age of Fable
> Had need to buckle on his belt.
> More game than he was ever able
> To take ran wild upon the veldt:

Each night with roast he stocked his table,
Then procreated on the pelt.
And that is how, of course, there came,
At last to be more men than game.

Upper Palaeolithic cave painting showing archers hunting stags. Cueva
de los Caballos, Albocácer, Castellón, Spain.
Fossil Man in Spain, *H. Obermaier, Yale University Press, 1924*

Man the Planter

There is probably some poetic license in Hope's humorous assessment of the hunter's happy situation, but at any rate the stage was set for the second population explosion, that of agriculture. Whether agriculture came because of population pressure, or population surged because of agriculture, is a moot point. British economist Colin Clark subscribes, tongue in check, to the former notion in his book *Population Growth and Land Use:*

It was probably increasing population density, or alternatively, in some areas, a change of climate, drying up the grasslands, which compelled our ancestors to take what was probably for them the very disagreeable step of commencing to live by agriculture. . . .

It was sometime in the Mesolithic Period, so far as we can ascertain, that the population of England had risen to nearly fifteen thousand, beyond the safe limit. We can imagine our ancestors having meetings about it, and saying that some birth restriction was necessary. There may have been some who advocated emigration to Scotland—this would have been ruled out as an altogether desperate expedient. Then there might have been some young man with a rather theoretical outlook, who suggested practising agriculture, something of which perhaps they had heard remotely, which was already established in Babylonia and Egypt. This obviously would have been ruled out as being quite impracticable in England. But agriculture eventually had to be adopted, with we can imagine how much reluctance, because increasing pressure of population simply left no alternative. For some generations, however—as in some parts of the world now—the men still regarded agricultural work so degrading that it could only be performed by women.

The magic of plants from seeds must have been discovered by accident, when grain brought in from some distance seeded and grew near the cave or camp. Gradually the fields were tilled, first by men and then by domesticated animals. Irrigation was also developed. About 10,000 years ago, then, the second population explosion took place when Cain and Abel split up, the former becoming a farmer rooted to his cultivated lands rather than a traditional nomad. And away went the census figures. In about 10,000 years the population increased a hundredfold, to 500 million. Instead of one person per ten square miles, ten were "crowded" into one square mile! Now there were 4,000 men for every one of Deevey's 125,000 at "dawn" a million years ago.

Whether or not the pressure of population had produced agriculture, agriculture definitely released the checks on population growth. For one thing, agriculture permitted the opening up of lands not previously habitable. And it was discovered that, generally speaking, plants themselves will support about ten times as many men as will the game that feed on those plants. With the "invention" of farming, a food-chain reaction went off around the world.

The Scientific Revolution

Had it not been for science and technology bringing the Industrial Revolution, today's population might be little more than it was 300 years ago. This is not to say that there would have been no overpopulation or hunger. These conditions doubtless existed in Stone Age days, and even in the later days of the agricultural revolution. If a square mile will support only ten people and for some reason fifteen are crowded into that area, trouble results. However, the Galileos and Newtons and Pasteurs and Faradays touched off the scientific revolution and the third population explosion began. Rather than treat this as a distinctly separate phenomenon from the agricultural revolution, we should probably consider that farming gave man the leisure necessary for the pursuit of science. As soon as it became possible for part of the population to feed all the population, some of those not involved in hunting or tilling the soil turned their restless and curious minds to other matters—with far-reaching results.

With books and guns and medicine, with steam engines and railroads and swift ships, men pushed out to new areas of the world—because of the population pressures at home. The first result of this expansion was the blessed room they sought; emancipated colonists could travel for days without seeing anyone. But population abhors a vacuum, and quickly grew to fill that vacuum. The third population explosion, fortunately, was not of the magnitude of the second. Thus far it is less than tenfold, although of course it has not been operating for the thousands of years the agricultural revolution had.

Not surprisingly, science and technology sparked a further agricultural revolution, with improved fertilizers and increased pest control. Today we have sophisticated techniques like genetic eradication by irradiation, causing sterility among male insects. Medicine has boosted population, and so have sanitation and life-saving techniques. Even war deaths have been affected, with battle losses fewer than in the old days before medical evacuation by helicopter and other aircraft became feasible. Transplants of organs and implants of artificial organs, still in infancy, bode to further increase the population, if only slightly.

For all these reasons there are now about sixteen people per square kilometer of earth's land surface, instead of the one per 250 kilometers a million years ago.

How Many Men?

Lest we think that because of the sparseness of population in primeval days not many of those men lived and died, Deevey estimates that some 36 billion Paleolithic or Stone Age humans lived. In all, about 110 billion humans are believed by Deevey to have preceded the 3.5 billion of us now on earth. Because of some 40,000 generations of men who lived before us, notwithstanding the few in each generation, between thirty and forty humans stand behind each one of us. As Deevey has pointed out, these numbers make it easy to understand all the stone tools and other relics constantly being turned up!

The Population Reference Bureau comes up with a somewhat different set of statistics, compiled by consultants Fletcher Wellmyer and Frank Lorimer, starting off with 600,000 B.C. as a take-off point for humankind. From that time to 6000 B.C. an estimated 12 billion people were born. Going back another million years would raise this figure to about 32 billion. Arriving at the end of the Stone Age, ready for the spurt caused by agriculture, the PRB estimate is from 5 to 10 million people then on Earth, compared with Deevey's figure of 5.3 million.

From 6000 B.C. to A.D. 1650, the wink of an eye compared to the hundreds of thousands of years to that point, population increased to 500 million, with some 42 billion births during the whole period. From the beginning of the scientific revolution to the present time, the PRB estimates a total number born of 23 billion. The PRB estimates also place the total human population ever to have lived at 77 billion, unless they go back another million years, in which case the total is 96 billion—more in agreement with Deevey, although the time factor differs quite a bit.

Now for the crux of all this research: For the Paleolithic period, growth was about 0.02 persons per thousand, annually; in the second period it rose to about 0.6 per thousand; and from then until now it has climbed to 4.35 per thousand. In the last three centuries population has tripled, and current growth is a full 2 percent a year, or 20 persons per thousand. "Explosion" is not too strong a word.

Man—A Slow Breeder

We recall that Deevey assigned man a population slot between the horse and the elephant. Charles Darwin, in *The Origin of Species*, said of the elephant, the slowest breeder:

. . . it will be safe to assume that it begins breeding when thirty years old, and goes on breeding till ninety years old, bringing forth six young in the interval, and surviving till one hundred years old; if this be so, after a period of from 740 to 750 years there would be nearly nineteen million elephants alive, descended from the first pair.

More fecund than the elephant, man is still "a slow-breeding organism of low fertility," as the biologist Hogben said. Our population problem does not stem from the fact that man is overly fertile. Compared with some other creatures, he is anything but that. Rats have demonstrated the ability to increase their numbers as much as twenty-fivefold in an average generation time, which is thirty-one weeks. And some water fleas make the rat look slow by comparison, with a two hundred twenty-onefold increase in a generation cycle of less than seven days!

According to T. H. Huxley, the offspring of a single aphid, if all lived, would in ten generations "contain more ponderable substance than 500 millions of stout men; that is, more than the whole population of China." G. W. Herrick estimated that a stem-mother cabbage aphid would produce 822 million tons of aphids during a period of four and a half months. Someone less meticulous has said if every codfish egg developed into an adult fish, the Atlantic Ocean would be packed solid in six years; such a fish locker might be handy to have. The Cymbidium orchid could fill the world with orchids in less than four generations; bacteria or protozoa could theoretically fill the universe in a few decades. None of these imaginative eventualities have come to pass, of course, because for various environmental reasons populations do not increase at their maximum potential.

Humans increase themselves at best by 1.4 times in a generation. Just as environment assumes that we are seldom up to our hips in rats or water fleas, until fairly recently in our existence environment also saw to it that man increased his numbers at a fairly slow rate. It is the death rate that throws the monkey wrench into things, and paradoxically humanitarianism has put us in the population-food bind. The United States, damned if it does or doesn't, seems to have done the most—both to create and ease the problem.

Explosion—American Style

When Columbus discovered the New World, North America had a population that has been estimated at about 1 million. The first U.S. census, in 1790, showed nearly 4 million people in the United States. For the next seventy years the increases per decade remained remarkably constant, ranging from 32.7 percent to 36.4 percent per decade. Since then they have gradually declined to the 18.5 percent increase shown in the 1960 census, with that for 1940 showing the lowest increase, 7.3 percent, attributed to the aftermath of the depression years. Since 1960 the rate of increase has continued to decline, and now stands at 0.8 percent a year, or about 8 percent a decade. Of the total increase since 1820, immigrants represent approximately one-fourth. At the first census in 1790 there were between 4 and 5 people per square mile. By 1860 there were 10.6 people per square mile in the United States, and the figure nationwide is now 50.5 per square mile. Alaska has about 1 person per square mile, Nevada has 2.5, and in Rhode Island the present density is 812 per mile. But the density of Chicago is 17,000 per mile, and for New York City it is 25,000 per mile, with 77,000 per mile in the borough of Manhattan!

The Birthrate

Dr. Samuel Johnson insisted to Boswell that the birthrate always remained constant, saying, "Births at all times bear the same proportion to the same number of people." In other words, women would have as many children as they were capable of having. Although this is no longer true in some developed countries, where birth control methods and cultural desires have drastically dropped the birthrate, worldwide this figure *has* historically been about the same, somewhat less than fifty per thousand women of childbearing age per year. This is a simple biological fact.

Women ovulate hundreds of times during a lifetime, but only a tiny fraction of these ovulations result in births. The world's record is thought to be held by Mrs. Bernard Scheinberg of Austria, with sixty-nine children. She was helped by having four sets of quadruplets, seven of triplets, and sixteen of twins! The odds against multiple births are 85 to 1 for twins, 7,629 to 1 for

The Author

DANIEL S. HALACY, JR., was born in Charleston, South Carolina, and attended schools there and in New England and California. During World War II and the Korean War, Mr. Halacy served in the Air Force. After graduation from Phoenix College and Arizona State University he was a technical writer and editor for several years and also taught writing at Phoenix College and Glendale Community College.

In 1962 Mr. Halacy left his position as Manager of the Technical Information Center at Motorola, in Phoenix, for full-time free-lance writing. He has published several hundred short stories and articles and a like amount of light verse and prose humor in a variety of magazines. His books have passed the fifty mark.

From 1966 to 1970 Mr. Halacy served as an Arizona senator, chairing the Education Committee and also serving on the Agriculture Committee. It was in the latter capacity that he began gathering the information for his new book, *The Geometry of Hunger.*

Mr. Halacy, a resident of Glendale, Arizona, is married and has two daughters.

72 73 74 75 10 9 8 7 6 5 4 3 2 1

by 1900. Today, as we have said, our expectancy in this country is over seventy years, and even that is exceeded by the Dutch.

It was the scientific revolution that was the most telling with respect to population increase. Life expectancy had slowly increased; after World War II it increased rapidly. For example, in Ceylon the death rate was about twenty-eight per thousand until pesticides were used against killer diseases like malaria. Almost immediately the death rate plummeted by half its amount to fourteen per thousand. With a birthrate of fifty per thousand, a death rate of twenty-eight leaves twenty-two per thousand net increase, a 2.2 percent increase a year. But cutting the death rate by fourteen lives per thousand leaves a 3.6 percent increase in population per year. By 1954 the death rate in Ceylon had dropped still further, to about ten, and since that time it has declined even more, to below nine per thousand. And this is not exceptionally low today. Here are some other death rates:

Taiwan	6
Hong Kong	5
Singapore	6
Reunion	4
Cyprus	7
Kuwait	6
Ryukyu Islands	5
Costa Rica	8
Cuba	8

Surprisingly, of 142 countries tabulated by the Population Reference Bureau, 36 have lower current death rates than the United States. Our rate is 9.7 per thousand, higher than that for many undeveloped countries.

The Compound-Interest Rate

One of Malthus's countrymen, Charles Babbage, who built a pioneering computer some 150 years ago, was well aware of the population increase, and felt it his duty to criticize two lines in Tennyson's poem "The Vision of Sin":

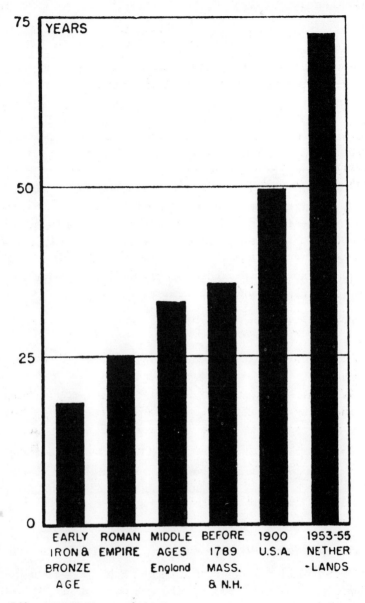

Life expectancy over the ages.
...ted with the permission of the Population Reference Bureau, Inc.

> Every minute dies a man,
> Every minute one is born.

Since this implied stability of population had *not* been achieved, Babbage wrote the following letter to Tennyson:

I need hardly point out to you that this calculation would tend to keep the sum total of the world's population in a state of perpetual equipoise, whereas it is a well-known fact that the said sum total is constantly on the increase. I would therefore take the liberty of suggesting that in the next edition of your excellent poem the erroneous calculation to which I refer be corrected as follows:

> Every moment dies a man
> And one and a sixteenth is born.

I may add that the exact figures are 1.067, but something must of course be conceded to meter.

Just what Tennyson thought of Babbage's criticism is unrecorded, but the poet did later make his work read:

> Every moment dies a man,
> Every moment one is born.

Which may or may not have pleased the literal-minded computer inventor.

With his claim that "one and a sixteenth is born," Babbage seemed to be assuming a 7 percent yearly increase in population. His father was a banker, and Babbage himself often worked up tables for banks and insurance companies, so he must have known what such an increase would lead to—the doubling of population in ten years instead of thirty-five.

There is one country, as a matter of fact, that presently has a population growth rate of even more than 7 percent. This is the tiny country of Kuwait, an oil-rich nation on the Persian Gulf. With a birthrate of 47 and a death rate of only 6, Kuwait shows an increase of 8.3. A good deal of this growth is because of immigration, however. Mercifully, Kuwait is unique in its growth rate and tiny in size.

Worldwide, the birthrate is thirty-four per thousand. The death rate is fourteen. Subtracting fourteen from thirty-four leaves twenty per thousand, a 2 percent increase globally a year. Of course the population increase is not the same in all countries. In the United States it is only about 0.8 percent. Northern Africa averages 3.1, Pakistan 3.3, Venezuela and Paraguay 3.4, and Costa Rica with a death rate of only eight and births of forty-five has a whopping 3.7 percent per year population growth, second highest in the world. At the low end are East Germany, enjoying a minimal 0.3 percent growth; Finland, Hungary, Belgium, and Austria, 0.4 percent; and the United Kingdom, 0.5 percent.

Over the years it has been observed that as death rates drop, so do birthrates. This is because people learn that it is no longer necessary to have five or six offspring to guarantee at least one son living into manhood. But the birthrate does not drop *immediately* —it generally takes many decades, even in a developed society. And today, Stone Age cultures with Stone Age birthrates have achieved modern death rates almost overnight. During the inevitable lag in birthrate reduction, population is soaring and will probably continue to do so for some time to come.

Mathematics is part of the problem, too—in the form of the geometrical progression 1, 2, 4, 8 . . . , the people half of the frightening Malthusian equation. When there werē a million of us on earth, a doubling meant only another million, and 2 million still rattled around in all those square miles. But doubling 1 *billion* makes 2 billion, and one more time reaches 4 billion—a population we are close to now. "Compound interest" at 2 percent a year doubles population with fantastic speed.

Benjamin Franklin was one of the early worriers over population increase, a concern that must have stemmed in part from his knowledge of the facts of life concerning compound interest. In 1791, putting this knowledge to work, Franklin bequeathed the sum of $5,000 to the citizens of Boston, with the proviso that the money be allowed to draw compound interest at 4½ percent for at least a century before any was used.

By 1891 the fund had grown to $322,000, at which time a portion was used for a school building. But this was only the beginning of the "money explosion." Within seventy years the fund had reached the huge sum of $17 million! Such proliferation of dollars is delightful—but when the compounded item is people the result is frightening.

It took us something like a million years to accumulate the first 3 billion humans. Now it appears that we will add another 3 billion in only thirty-five years, about 3/10,000 as long a time!

People in the mass.
Courtesy of Planned Parenthood Federation of America, Inc.

We have met the enemy and they are us.

Pogo

CHAPTER 3

Birth Control and Death Control

Certainly we must prefer some sensible form of birth control to the more drastic eventualities that may limit world population otherwise. We have achieved great success in death control—such great success that it now demands a countering control of birth. How fares the nation, and the world, in this balancing act? At best the situation is confused. At worst it presents one of the most difficult problems facing us. There is good reason for this difficulty.

The fact that there are many causes of death but only one of birth would seem to make the problem of birth control an easy one. However, our thoughts and feelings about death are very different from those about birth. No one has to be told that death must be controlled. But few people have the same convictions about birth control.

The History of Birth Control

Various contraceptive methods were known and practiced by primitive peoples. Physical and chemical birth control techniques were used by the Romans; some writers choose to link such measures with the fall of the Empire. France was perhaps the first modern country to use contraceptives widely, as indicated by the drastic reduction of population growth there in Malthus's time. Induced abortion has also long been resorted to for prevention of unwanted births. Such measures ranged from crude physical means such as jumping from a chair, or even a roof, to the use of chemicals or crude surgery with sticks or other instruments.

Despite this long and ample precedent, however, the birth control "movement" can be said to have truly started in England, shortly following Malthus's dire warnings of population excesses. By 1832 an American named Charles Knowlton had written a pamphlet, "The Fruits of Philosophy," describing contraceptive measures. The path of such pioneers was difficult, however, and their material was branded obscene and often seized forthwith by the authorities. As late as 1877 Annie Besant and Charles Bradlaugh were tried for selling Knowlton's pamphlets. The attendant publicity helped the founding of the Malthusian League, and in 1878 the first birth control clinic was founded in Holland by Aletta Jacobs. Not until 1921 was a similar clinic set up in London, mainly through the dedicated efforts of Dr. Marie Stopes.

When Margaret Sanger opened her clinic in Brooklyn in 1916, it was promptly closed down by the police and Mrs. Sanger was sentenced to twenty days in jail for her efforts. Undaunted, she formed the first birth control organization in the United States, the Birth Control League. By 1923 she was able to set up a permanent clinic. Slowly her efforts succeeded, and restrictions against contraceptive devices were liberalized, beginning in the late 1920s. In 1936 laws against mailing birth control information were eased. Court rulings slowly eroded state legislation against contraceptive use: by 1960 only Massachusetts and Connecticut continued to enforce, or attempt enforcement of, laws against dissemination of birth control information.

Writer Karl Sax, in his book *Standing Room Only*, pointed out that fortunately there were many scofflaws in Connecticut:

Margaret Sanger.
Wide World Photos

If, for example, the people of Connecticut obeyed the law in that state which prohibits the practice of birth control, the birth rate might well reach 40 per thousand even in a relatively mature population. With modern death rates of 10 per thousand, the population would increase in a century from little more than 2 million to more than 32 million, and in two centuries would reach 500 million. In another hundred years the population of the little state would reach 8,000 million, if enough standing room could be found.

In 1961 a birth control clinic was closed in New Haven, and this led to the law being challenged in the U.S. Supreme Court. By 1970 holdout Massachusetts legalized birth control measures. At present most churches accept birth control, although the Roman Catholic Church still forbids any method but the rhythm system.

Ecologist Garrett Hardin has taken Pope Paul to task for "fiddling while the world breeds" and suggesting that the rhythm method (which Hardin referred to as "Roman roulette") not be indulged in "too often." Hardin likens the Vatican's actions to those taken against Galileo, but fears that, unlike the recanting that took place in the Galileo case after 189 years, the Roman Catholic Church will never change its stand on birth control.

Meanwhile, it seems fairly common knowledge that many individual Catholics—even Italians in the shadow of the Vatican—avail themselves of various birth control methods, including particularly "the pill." And it was a Catholic—Dr. John Rock—who invented the pill.

Birth Control Methods

There are a variety of methods of birth control. Chastity is an obvious one, and its implementation has been called for by such noted figures as Mahatma Gandhi and Pope Paul, among many. Such continence is obviously difficult of achievement, humans still being endowed with the passions Malthus was so well aware of. Short of a total physical separation of men from women, birth control through continence is an idealistic dream—and unnecessarily heartless as well.

The rhythm system, intercourse only on "safe" days, marked on the calendar and double-checked with a thermometer, is a more workable solution. It is also obviously not fully effective as a birth control method.

Coitus interruptus, the method chosen by Onan to keep his seed from his brother's wife, is practiced by many, despite the fears of some that it leads to frustration and other ills on the part of the male. The fact that God struck Onan dead is used as an argument against the practice, although a closer look indicates that God punished Onan for failure to obey, rather than for the particular method he used in being disobedient.

The condom and the diaphragm are probably the most effective artificial contraceptive measures and, barring occasional accidental mishap, approach 100 percent effectiveness. More recently there have been new developments, notably "the pill" and "the loop," or intrauterine device (IUD). Available now for several years, the pill, which inhibits ovulation, has been credited with about 25 percent of the reduction in births in the United States. There are some side effects, interestingly including the apparent increased probability of conception when the pill is discontinued, as well as some possibility of harmful physiological results. However, it is reasonable to expect improvements, perhaps of great magnitude: one pill that may take care of a whole month, pills for males, and so on.

The IUD, which has a fairly long history, is an improvement on the diaphragm. Cheap to make and easy to insert "permanently," it is generally quite effective. The popular "Lippes loop," named for its developer, Dr. Jack Lippes, is produced in many countries for a few cents each, and is part of the global arsenal against unwanted population.

There are more drastic methods of birth control. Castration has been practiced for ages for various purposes. Sterilization is a gentler operation; many males have it done when they no longer desire children, and female sterilization is also effective. Unfortunately, forced sterilization of criminals and the mentally deficient has given a black eye to the technique. More seriously, it is drastic and irreversible surgery, although in some cases children have been born after such operations—in which cases a fair-minded surgeon should pick up the tab. However, experimental work is being done on a reversible male sterilization method. Instead of cutting the vas deferens, as in present surgery, the doctor ties it off with a clip that may be removed later.

Primitive peoples practiced infanticide and abortion mainly because other birth control techniques were not available to them. Primitive tribes still practice abortion much as it was practiced in prehistoric times, and Hippocrates, Aristotle, and Plato recommended abortion to limit population and thus keep an economically sound society. Chinese writings of 4,600 years ago describe the use of mercury to effect abortions; "bush tea" has also been used, as has phosphorus, and more recently hormones have been tried. But while chemical methods have persisted, in spite of their general failure, physical methods are more effective.

There seems no question of the efficacy of abortion as a means of birth control; it is credited with quickly reducing population growth in Japan after World War II. Large numbers of abortions are also performed in South Korea and Taiwan. In Europe West Germany, Hungary, and Czechoslovakia permit abortions. Some countries that do not permit them legally still estimate more abortions than live births. In France and Italy, for example, up to a million abortions a year are estimated. Romania and Bulgaria found abortions too effective in lowering the birthrate, and made legal abortions more difficult to obtain.

England, where abortion was not a crime until 1803, now has legalized abortions, but only about 50,000 a year are performed, including several thousand on women from other countries. Sweden also permits legal abortions, although surprisingly few are performed, the total for a recent year being about 10,000.

In the United States, where, surprisingly, abortion was not considered a crime until 1830, abortion laws are very strict in most states. But because today there are many who see abortion as the answer to our population problems, the laws of many states are being changed to permit abortions more readily—in some cases on a completely permissive basis.

Just how "therapeutic" an abortion is remains a question. Removal of a fetus up to several months old is surely a more serious operation than surgical sterilization, which, incidentally, would obviate the need for many abortions. Abortions take longer, require more skill, and are potentially more dangerous, without going into the possible psychic scars that may never heal. These may be among the reasons that abortion is still illegal for nearly two-thirds of the world's population.

Sex and Hunger

Perhaps the weirdest birth control theory was expounded by a man who should have known better. Brazilian Josue de Castro, when he was chairman of the United Nations Food and Agriculture Organization, made the following hyperbolic statement in his book, *The Geography of Hunger:*

Hunger is responsible for the overproduction of human beings, excessive in number and inferior in quality, who are hurled blindly into the demographic metabolism of the world.

Thoroughly convinced of this fantastic explanation, de Castro advanced as an argument the fact that people in developed nations had fewer children. From this he reasoned that hunger somehow acted to make the hungry more fertile.

Actually, as common sense would indicate, the fact is that those in advanced countries *choose* to have fewer children. New Zealanders eat eight times as much meat as the Japanese but have a similar birthrate. Eskimos consume more protein than any other ethnic group, 45 percent of that being animal protein, but their birthrate of forty-seven per thousand is among the highest in the world. Experiments with rats showed those fed more milk were five times as fertile as those fed a lesser amount. And city rats have been described as being larger than poorly fed country rats but more than twice as fertile.

Here was a man obviously thinking with his heart rather than his head. However, such an emotional approach to the problem of birth control and hunger can do little to advance a solution. As has been demonstrated, feeding the hungry peoples results in an increase in the growth rate, rather than the decrease de Castro foresaw.

The "Antinatalists"

The following was among material presented by the Colombo Plan Consultative Committee at the Senate "Population Crisis" hearings in February, 1968:

Family planning, birth control, and contraception have been widely accepted in the United States for at least 35 years. With a large majority of adults participating, the society has engaged, in effect, in an

TRENDS IN U.S. VITAL RATES,
NATURAL INCREASE

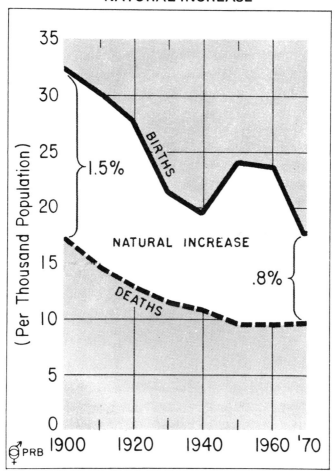

Though the U.S. rate of natural increase has dropped off markedly since 1960, it still accounts for over 1.6 million additional Americans (not including net migration) each year. Sources: *Vital Statistics Report 1967*, National Center for Health Statistics, Department of HEW; *Monthly Vital Statistics Report*, September 30, 1969.

Reprinted with the permission of the Population Reference Bureau, Inc.

informal population program on its own initiative—a program in
which each individual decides whether and under what circumstances
to participate. The methods of control uses include the full range of
those available—mainly the diaphragm and jelly, the condom, sterilization, and the rhythm method. Millions of women have begun to
use contraceptive pills since their development a few years ago, and
many thousands are now being attracted to the intrauterine device.

The main body of the public has long been convinced of the need
for family limitation, has known of the available methods, has had
supplies and medical services readily available, and has been economically able to obtain these from suppliers and private physicians.
Thus, the setting for family planning has been strikingly different
from that of the less developed countries.

In the United States and many other countries, it can hardly
be lack of knowledge about birth control that prevents reduction
in population. It is easy to lead someone to water, but something
else again to make him drink at the birth control spring of knowledge, particularly since there is relatively little starvation in the
United States, and much affluence. There are, however, loud cries
from many quarters that we must curb our population. For some
alarmists the already appreciable reduction in our growth rate is
too little and perhaps too late.

While it is undeniable that world population is soaring, it is
also true that in some countries population growth is minimal and
perhaps not more than such countries can handle. In the United
States, which has a relatively low growth rate and is the most
affluent of nations, there is nevertheless a loud and growing demand that Zero Population Growth be achieved—by any means,
according to some, from "free and easy" abortions to enforced
sterilization. While most advocates of compulsory birth control
are doubtless sincere and serious, many are far from logical or
scientific, and may well be embarrassed in years ahead as they
recall their blasts against motherhood and the family.

The militant Zero Population Growth organization was
launched at Yale University in 1968, and by the end of 1969 had
recruited some 3,000 members. A goal of 10,000 was set for 1970.
A prime mover in the organization is biology professor Paul

Ehrlich of Stanford, one of the most vocal of doomsaying ecologists. Without population curbs, he says in *U.S. News & World Report*, March 2, 1970, ". . . there's just no hope that civilization will persist."

The "antinatalists" come out foursquare for all methods of limiting population, from sterilization to pills to abortion, with most accent on abortion. Their goal is not more than 2.1 children per family on the average, a figure aimed at stabilizing United States population at about 250 million by the year 2010. How effective the ZPGers will be remains to be seen; whether cold logic can triumph over natural passion and the urge to procreate is doubtful. Meanwhile, long-time birth control advocates are concerned that the extremists like Ehrlich and other ZPG militants may cause a "birth backlash" that could hurt the whole program.

In 1969 presidential counsel John Erlichman was warned by doctors Garrett Hardin and Donald Aitken—apparently speaking for some thirty other conferees assembled at the first meeting of the Muir Institute, one of the recent proliferation of "conservation" groups—that the official federal notion of limiting population by voluntary birth control was "insanity," and that birth control would have to be made compulsory to avert the chaos of threatened global overpopulation.

According to Hardin: "In the long run, voluntarism is insanity. The result will be continued uncontrolled population growth." Aitken was more specific: "The government has to step in and tamper with religious and personal convictions—and maybe even impose penalties for every child a family has beyond two."

It is easy to say, as presidential advisers are saying volubly now, that voluntary birth control just won't get the job done. It is somewhat more difficult to implement a program of compulsory population reduction. While some seem to be clamoring for an army of occupation to invade the very beds of overpopulaters and perhaps sterilize all offending males, it is difficult to see how coercion can actually be used. Who is brave enough to forcibly sterilize or abort alleged "popullution" offenders? There have al-

ready been charges that birth control pills and other curbs have
been forced on poor women who did not want them. On this
particular point Dr. Jean Mayer, the President's adviser on food,
made a startling statement in the summer 1969 issue of *Columbia
Forum:*

> Rich people occupy much more space, consume more of each
> natural resource, disturb the economy more, and create more land,
> air, water, chemical, thermal and radioactive pollution than poor peo-
> ple. So it can be argued that from many viewpoints it is even more
> urgent to control the numbers of the rich than it is to control the
> numbers of the poor.

Understandably, most antinatalists hedge on the matter of coercion, or at least try to soft-pedal that approach. In the words of
Dr. Judith Blake, chairman of the University of California's
demography department, in *Science,* May 2, 1969:

> Anti-natalist policies will not necessarily involve the introduction
> of coercive measures. In fact, just the opposite is the case. Many of
> these new policies will entail a lifting of pressures to reproduce,
> rather than an imposition of pressures not to do so.

Tying the concept of ZPG with the burgeoning "women's
liberation" movement, some antinatalists claim that women have
children simply because they have nothing constructive to do and
that when they are guaranteed the right to a rewarding career
they will in many cases not even want children! It is doubtful
that the most determined feminist can change the instincts toward
motherhood and family that are our genetic and cultural heritage.
It is doubtful, too, that some women will ever feel any career
more rewarding than a family.

A variety of other reasons are advanced to help sell the idea of
curbing the crop of babies in the United States. Oddly, in the
face of our increased affluence, Robert C. Cooke wrote in *Population Bulletin,* August 1966:

> One thing is certain: there was a time in the good old days when
> "cheaper by the dozen" had a plausible social and financial basis. Few

couples are so favorably endowed that they can provide the emotional security and intellectual challenge required to give each child of a "cheaper by the dozen" brood the rich stimulating environment essential for individual development.

The Carrot and the Stick

If voluntarism won't work, there are those who would pass legislation that will. Such bills include the remarkable SB 1421 introduced by Nadao Yoshinaga in the Hawaiian legislature in 1970:

FIFTH LEGISLATURE, 1970
STATE OF HAWAII   S.B. No 1421-70

A BILL FOR AN ACT

Relating to population control.

BE IT ENACTED BY THE LEGISLATURE OF THE STATE OF HAWAII:

SECTION 1. The legislature finds: (1) that population growth is the most serious and most challenging problem for mankind today; (2) that the time necessary for the population of the world to double is now about thirty-five years; (3) that the "death rate solution" by war, famine, or pestilence is an unacceptable destructive solution to the problem of population growth; and (4) that population control is an acceptable humanitarian solution to the problem of population growth.

The purpose of this Act is to control the population size of this State by a program of birth regulation.

SECTION 2. Every physician attending a woman resident of this State at the time she is giving birth in the State shall, if the woman has two or more living children, perform such medical technique or operation as will render the woman sterile.

SECTION 3. This Act shall take effect on July 1, 1971.

INTRODUCED BY: Nadao Yoshinaga

This drastic bill, coming hot on the heels of Hawaii's permissive abortion bill, did not pass but is nevertheless an indication of the thinking of some that population control can be legislated. It is doubtful that the voting public is yet ready for this sort of birth control, particularly since provision in England for free abortions and the introduction of compulsory sterilization legislation elsewhere raise the fear in some minds that euthanasia can't be far behind.

Approaching population control in a different and certainly more palatable manner, Senator Robert Packwood of Oregon introduced in Congress a bill that would provide federal tax exemptions for the first two children of any couple, but none for additional offspring. However, such legislation would have no effect on rich parents—and none on the poor either, since they would pay little if any tax at any rate. Packwood admits that even its effect on middle-class families is uncertain and that perhaps the bill would only be symbolic legislation, ". . . a government commitment to make an effort to achieve stabilization."

Surprisingly, Senator George McGovern, generally considered one of the leading environmentalists in government, in 1970 favored legislation giving sixty-five dollars a month for each child in "guaranteed income" plans. Such a measure could hardly help the cause of population control. There is a flurry of other legislation, at the national and state levels, aimed at making small families, or even no families at all, popular. And pressure continues for the legalization of homosexuality, as a weapon for population control.

Forgetting for the moment the question of whether or not a policy of government regulation of births would be wise ecologically, consider its more immediate effect on the population at large. Such is the human spirit that, being told we can't legally have intoxicating liquor, we get it illegally. Perhaps being told we can have only 2.1 children per family, we might perversely set out to show Uncle Sam or whoever how wrong he is!

As late as the early nineteenth century, United States women were producing babies at a figure close to the physiological upper limit. By the mid-thirties this had dropped a drastic two-thirds, to about seventeen per thousand of population, where it is again today. Translated into numbers, births per woman dropped from between eight and ten in the early days to about three by 1920, and just over two in the depression days. Interestingly, the Population Reference Bureau has this to say about the drop in the United States birthrate:

So significant a change had nothing to do with governmental policies calculated to encourage a decrease in fertility. It was due to a spontaneous readjustment of family size as mortality declined and life expectation increased.

Daniel P. Moynihan put it this way on CBS "Face the Nation," January 25, 1970:

There is no government in history that has ever had any effect whatever on population. . . . One of the nice things about people is that they don't pay too much attention to Government . . . particularly with respect to the number of children they have.

Some Jews and Russian kulaks might question the first part of his statement; however, this simply serves to make Moynihan's point more telling.

The natural urge to have children seems much more ingrained, much more sacred and zealously guarded—instinctively if not otherwise—than the right to vote, bear arms, or attend the college of one's own choice. The desire—conscious or unconscious—to use children as a means to achieve our immortality is a strong factor. So are religious beliefs and ancient customs and mores. Perhaps strongest of all is the natural "right to bear children," a right it will be difficult to amend by government order.

The "Pronatalists"

For all the antinatalists, there are pronatalists who outnumber them, and who also have powerful weapons on their side, not the least of which is our natural love for children. To hear some antinatalists talk one would get the idea that most children were unwanted, illegitimate, or careless little accidents. However, through history it is safe to say that children are generally loved. To a large extent they are deliberately produced to be loved.

Sex—that is, the gender of the offspring—is another factor favoring more children. Often two youngsters would suffice if they could be of the sex desired by their parents. Should the day come when sex can be influenced prenatally without harmful side effects, birth control will have gained a powerful tool.

Actually, population growth in the United States and many other developed lands is not all that bad. In fact our birthrate, presently at an all-time low, will perhaps sink even lower with improvements in birth control methods, continuing education, and so on. If we cannot achieve zero growth with all these things going for us, what of the developing nations? It is there that the population picture is truly bleak. Our own rate of increase is less than 1 percent currently. Worldwide it is 2 percent, and in the most depressed areas the increase is 3 percent and more. Costa Rica, for example, with a per capita GNP of only $405, has a

3.7 percent population increase per year, enough to raise it more than thirtyfold in a single century!

Unfortunately, in the depressed nations the historic need to have many children (to guarantee a living son of mature years to provide for aging parents) still operates, even with drastically lowered death rates.

Global Birth-Controllers

In a treatise on population, demographer Kingsley Davis comments in *Scientific American*, September 1963:

. . . others are struggling with the handicap of a population growth greater than any industrializing country had to contend with in the past. A number of them now realize that this is a primary problem, and their governments are pursuing or contemplating pursuing large-scale programs of birth-limitation. They are receiving little help in this matter, however, from the industrial nations, which have so willingly helped them to lower their death rates.

Dr. Lee DuBridge, science adviser to President Nixon, voiced a similar sentiment to a UNESCO conference, November 25, 1969:

Can we not invent a way to reduce our population growth to zero? Every human institution—school, university, church, family, government and international agency such as UNESCO—should set this as its prime task.

Such remarks must come as a shock to those who for decades *have* tried diligently to help nations needing birth control information, such as the Rockefeller and Ford foundations, Sweden's SIDA organization, and many others, including our AID program, which even has a "loop corps" out in the field pushing IUDs. The population explosion has not come about simply because no one sought to help in the area of birth control.

Decades ago Margaret Sanger did her utmost, not just in the United States but in foreign countries as well, to sell the controversial idea of birth control. She was perhaps the most well-known such missionary, but she was by no means alone in her

efforts. The Pathfinder Fund began family planning activities in
the United States in 1929. In 1952 it expanded its activities to
countries on four other continents, and by 1967 it had helped set
up twenty-four national family planning associations. More recently it has been analyzing data on the use and effects of IUDs
in eighty-two countries around the world.

The International Planned Parenthood Federation was founded
in 1952. At present it has fifty-four organizations in foreign countries, and its services have been given to a total of more than
seventy countries. The Population Council was founded, also in
1952, by John D. Rockefeller III. It has staff members in eleven
foreign countries, and aids family-planners in a number of other
lands. The Ford Foundation has provided more than $90 million
since 1952 in the United States and overseas for birth control
work. Of that, $45 million went for reproductive biology studies
to develop better contraceptives. The Rockefeller Foundation
has spent $14 million since 1964, and in 1967 the Population
Council had a budget of $10 million.

Other birth control organizations active globally include the
International Planned Parenthood Federation, the Brush Foundation, the Milbank Fund, the Oxford Committee for Famine Relief
(OXFAM), the Victor Fund, CARE, the Church World Service,
Lutheran World Relief, the Mennonite Central Committee, the
Unitarian Universalist Service Committee, Inc., and World Neighbors. Sweden, the United Kingdom, Denmark, Norway, Japan,
and the Netherlands also give help where requested, with Sweden
alone spending $9 million in 1968.

It is easy to find fault and to lay blame, much easier than it is
to find ways of doing something about the problems of population. Even assuming that we have all the right answers as to who
should have how many children, implementing these decisions
takes some doing. For example, many of the countries most needing birth control fight hardest against any concrete action in this
direction—surely a clue! When the matter was brought up in the
United Nations, some members challenged the propriety of even

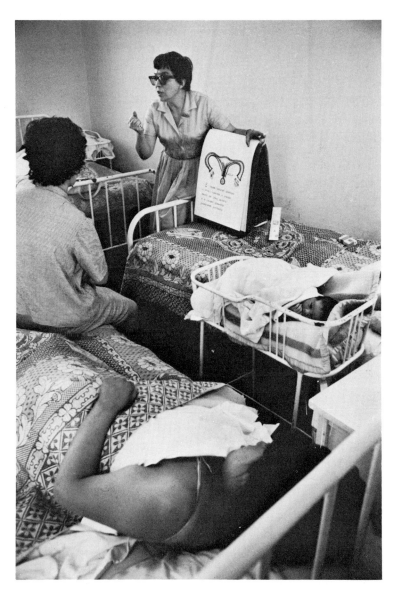

Birth control program in Santiago, Chile, is given in hospital to new mothers at a particularly receptive time.
The Rockefeller Foundation

discussing such "intimate matters." Not until 1967 was a policy statement formulated, and it was signed by only 30 of the 126 member nations.

In December 1967 the following countries signed a "Declaration on World Population": Colombia, Finland, India, Korea, Malaysia, Morocco, Nepal, Singapore, Sweden, Tunisia, the United Arab Republic, Yugoslavia, Australia, Barbados, Denmark, the Dominican Republic, Ghana, Japan, Jordan, Indonesia, Iran, The Netherlands, New Zealand, Norway, Pakistan, the Philippines, Thailand, Trinidad-Tobago, the United Kingdom, and the United States, with President Johnson signing for our country. Here were thirty nations, representing something more than one-third of the world's population, subscribing, at least in principle, to the following:

DECLARATION ON WORLD POPULATION

The peace of the world is of paramount importance to the community of nations, and our governments are devoting their best efforts to improving the prospects for peace in this and succeeding generations. But another great problem threatens the world, a problem less visible but no less immediate. That is the problem of unplanned population growth.

It took mankind all of recorded time until the middle of the last century to achieve a population of one billion. Yet it took less than a hundred years to add the second billion, and only thirty years to add the third. At today's rate of increase, there will be four billion people by 1975 and nearly seven billion by the year 2000. This unprecedented increase presents us with a situation unique in human affairs and a problem that grows more urgent with each passing day.

The numbers themselves are striking, but their implications are of far greater significance. Too rapid population growth seriously hampers efforts to raise living standards, to further education, to improve health and sanitation, to provide better housing and transportation, to forward cultural and recreational opportunities—and even in some countries to assure sufficient food. In short, the human aspiration, common to men everywhere, to live a better life is being frustrated and jeopardized.

As heads of governments actively concerned with the population problem, we share these convictions:

WE BELIEVE that the population problems must be recognized as a principal element in long-range national planning if governments are to achieve their economic goals and fulfill the aspirations of their people.

WE BELIEVE that the opportunity to decide the number and spacing of children is a basic human right.

WE BELIEVE that lasting and meaningful peace will depend to a considerable measure upon how the challenge of population growth is met.

WE BELIEVE that the objective of family planning is the enrichment of human life, not its restriction; that family planning, by assuring greater opportunity to each person, frees man to attain his individual dignity and reach his full potential.

Recognizing that family planning is in the vital interest of both the nation and the family, we, the undersigned, earnestly hope that leaders around the world will share our views and join with us in this great challenge for the well-being and happiness of people everywhere.

Conspicuously absent among the signatories were the Soviet Union and other Communist nations, although it was hardly expected that they would subscribe to the family planning declaration. Karl Marx was one of the loudest in damning Malthusian theories, and the party line has not basically changed. The Communists claim that famous chemist Dmitri Mendeleev long ago demonstrated that Malthus was wrong when he stated in his "Essay on the Principle of Population": "As population increases, science and technology will make it possible to utilize all the newer and newer strivings previously unknown to man." Nevertheless, it is estimated that in the 1930s the number of abortions in Moscow exceeded the live births.

Russia continually rails against the "neo-Malthusians," and brings charges of "cannibalism" and "infanticide" against the West. But Russia, who lost 5 million kulaks when Stalin collectivized the farms, and perhaps as many as 40 million during World War II, was faced with a problem of serious underpopulation—hence, such statements as this one of Lavrenti Beria in 1951 at the 34th anniversary celebration of the Soviet Union:

Whereas, in the camp of the capitalists, the imperialist cannibals are employed in inventing various "scientific" means for wiping out the better part of humanity and reducing the birth rate, in our country Comrade Stalin has said, "People are the most precious capital and their well-being and happiness are the government's great concern."

From 1950 to 1960 Russia grew about as fast as the United States, however, and has recently and quietly relegalized abortions and cut subsidy payments to large families and illegitimate children. Thus, while the Communists ostensibly reject birth control —Romania, for instance, tightened up on birth control in 1966, permitting its birthrate to jump from 14 to 39 by August of 1967 —Russia dropped her birthrate from 25 in 1960 to 18.2 in 1966.

Russia's P. G. Podyachikh, speaking at the U.N. Economic and Social Council Population Commission in 1965, said: "While certain countries might experience food shortage in particular years, in the long run it is possible—many experts believe—to feed not only the present world population but a population one hundred times greater."

Bounds of Decency

Opposition to birth control is not all on ideological grounds. Understandably, the whole question remains a touchy one with many peoples. Shrouded for ages in inhibitions stemming from religion and moral beliefs, as well as superstition and downright ignorance, attitudes on reproduction are difficult to discuss, much less change in a few years. Only very recently has the United States had the forthrightness to advocate population curbs. President Eisenhower pointed out that this was a subject for individual decision, and President Kennedy went little further. Only with Lyndon Johnson did government break precedent and urge family planning. Johnson on the twentieth anniversary of the U.N. in 1965 said: "Let us in all lands—including this land—face forthrightly the multiplying problems of our multiplying populations and seek answers to the most profound challenge to the future of all the world."

Ernest Michanek, director general of the Swedish International Development Authority, expressed the belief during the 1966 Senate "Population Crisis" hearing that it is: ". . . a human right for all parents to plan the size of their families—including the case of subfertility—and to be assisted with a view to getting the number of children they can provide for." Such a statement can hardly be faulted. Senator Ernest Gruening, chairman of the "Population Crisis" hearings, subscribed to it and enlarged upon it as follows in the 1968 continuation of hearings:

We have no right to reserve this knowledge for a few. On the contrary, we are under obligation to disseminate it—for ethical reasons, for reasons of morale, for social reasons, and—let us not forget— economic reasons. As you know, the Congress last session, aware of population pressures, earmarked $35 million for family planning in the foreign aid bill.

Here is where the concept of family planning gets into serious trouble, however. Regardless of how the President felt, or how the legislature felt, many charged with implementing our foreign aid programs refuse to take any but the most permissive attitude with regard to birth control programs. To Senator Gruening, AID Director William S. Gaud explained the organization's philosophy:

Population policy is based on four fundamental principles.
First, that overpopulation and underdevelopment go hand in hand.
Second, that the government of every nation with a population problem should do its utmost to increase knowledge of family planning. Our rule is to encourage and help developing nations in this task.
Third is respect for the sovereignty and sensibilities of the nations we assist. The population question is as delicate as it is urgent. Section 291 of the Foreign Assistance Act of 1967 says "every nation is and should be free to determine its own policies and procedures with respect to problems of population growth and family planning within its own boundary."

Four, AID supports no family planning or population program unless it is voluntary. We want no part of either international coercion or individual coercion. We do not make family planing a condition of aid.

Confronted with a previous policy statement by President Johnson that: "The position of the United States of America is clear. We will give our help and our support to nations which make their own decisions to insure an effective balance between the numbers of their people and the food they have to eat," Director Gaud's response was:

. . . I do not buy the proposition that we should make such a program a condition of aid. It just seems to me that that is unwise, that the whole question of family planning and population control is a very delicate personal business. . . . If the richest, largest, and most powerful nation in the world says to its poverty-stricken neighbors, "I will not give you any help to feed and educate your people unless you carry out a population control program," I think that would be most unwise.

Before writing off Gaud as an unrealistic bureaucrat, consider sample comments on family planning from a few foreign countries:

Monseigneur Hector Enrique Santos, Archbishop of Tegucigalpa: "A foreign government which conditions its aid by programs of this kind is not a friend but an enemy which seeks to reduce us to permanent impotence."

The Archbishop of Costa Rica: "It would be interesting to find out how many thousands of dollars have been invested in Costa Rica in that campaign of disorientation and disrespect for human dignity."

The Apostolic Administrator of Colombia (which nation was the first signer of the Declaration on World Population): ". . . a flagrant violation of the Rights of Man expressed in the United Nations Charter."

A Cartegena priest: "Any nation accepting such conditions [birth control] enslaves in man the freest act in nature."

New York Times journalist James Reston complained bitterly in his paper on April 9, 1967, about:

> . . . [the] stubborn vanity and stupidity of the ignorant male in Latin America . . . worse than the baboon and worships the cult of virility long after he has forgotten the cult of Christianity. . . . The Latin male is not satisfied with love, he must have life, one new life a year, if possible, in order to prove he is good for something.

Perhaps Reston was among those who were not appreciative of President Kennedy's brother Robert, then father of nine, quoted as saying in Peru: "I challenge any of you to produce more children than I have!"

In Latin America the birth-controllers apparently run afoul of everybody, including the Roman Catholic Church, of course—particularly in view of the encyclical *Humanae Vitae*. The revolutionaries are said to reject birth control as a "Malthusian palliative designed to distract attention from the ulterior motives of capitalistic economy," and conservative Latins lean on their nationalistic tendencies and fear population control as a "colonial attempt to emasculate the awakening Latin American culture."

On June 21, 1963, El Salvador's *Diario de Hoy* phrased this warning against birth control:

> They plan to destroy the capital of Latin America, to frighten away private investment, to socialize us before we have capitalized, and to block our growth, slashing the wombs of Latin mothers, castrating Latin males, before we have grown sufficiently or taken possession of the vast empty lands of the continent.

Even liberal social reformers, warmest to the idea, are leery that perhaps "bargain-loving United States will substitute Lippes loops for agrarian reform," according to Dr. J. Mayore Stycos in *Population Reference Bureau*, No. 26, January 1969. Against odds like this, selling birth control abroad is no easy thing. Add to it minor frustrations like those of the single Peace Corps worker asked by suspicious native women how she knew all about contraceptives, and of the ignorant woman given a "fertility rosary" of colored beads since she had no calendar—and who thought all she had to do was move the beads on successive days to prevent pregnancy!

Mission Not Accomplished

Despite all sorts of opposition, however, family-planners have persevered. In addition to the millions in private funds, the U.S. government in 1967 spent $28 million, in 1968 $41 million, and in 1969 $61 million on birth control. More millions were spent for that purpose in foreign aid, $35 million in 1967 alone. In 1967 the developed countries had 10 million women on oral contraceptives, the developing countries some 3 million. Seventeen developing nations are carrying out government-supported family planning, and forty others have voluntary organizations. AID has financed population planning in some thirty countries, and in 1967, for the first time, AID spent money for contraceptive "hardware" in developing nations.

If success were being achieved, it would be easier to swallow the abuse heaped on those who would "impose" birth control on the world. Unfortunately, it seems that even minimal success is not at hand. A case in point is India. AID Director Gaud said in February 1968 before a Senate hearing: "The Indian Government has had a national family planning policy and program since 1951. It has not been a dynamic or effective program. But now, under vigorous leadership from a new Family Planning Minister, the program appears to be moving." More than 1 million IUDs had been inserted in Indian women by the end of 1967, 40,000 women were taking pills, and voluntary sterilization was increasing, with 23,000 operations in a single month. But the most recent figures show India's population increase up from 2.5 percent in 1967 to 2.6 percent in 1969!

Gaud was also high in his praise of Premier Ayub of Pakistan, a diligent worker for population control. Ayub's goal was to reduce the whopping birthrate of fifty per thousand to forty by 1970. Sadly, by 1969 the figure had already climbed to fifty-two.

In their book, *Famine—1975*, the Paddocks bitterly describe the false hope of the pill and failure of the IUD. Even Dr. Lippes seems to despair of the overwhelming logistics problem. India had planned to insert 3 million loops in 1966 and 6 million in 1967. But at last reports 25 million would have to be inserted in a single year to stem the baby tide. At best, teams can do one insertion each six minutes, or eighty per working day. Complicating the problem is the objection of many women to male doctors doing the work. There are only 8,000 women doctors in India, and of course there is more for them to do than just insert IUDs. Even the sterilization program that had looked hopeful is making little dent, despite free operations, holidays with pay, and cash bonuses both for the patient and the man who brought him in.

To those who pointed to Japan's success, the Paddocks were curt. Japan's people had been literally pushed to the wall, with a 1968 population density of 685 per square mile; even "crowded" India is only half the Japanese density. The Japanese are highly literate, with a rate of 98 percent as far back as 1948 (by comparison Latin America is 60 percent literate and Africa only 16 percent). Additionally, the Japanese accept abortions with no qualms and have a large and skilled medical profession to perform such operations. Despite all this, however, the Japanese population is still increasing faster than that of the United States.

In frustration, those favoring birth control point out the sham of family planning that simply means that a couple decides how many children they will have, and the irony in the fact that most of those seeking counsel *already have more than four children!* Worldwide, the number of children per family is 4.6. In the developing regions it is 5.4, in developed regions 2.9; in North America it is 3.7, in Europe 2.7, and in the Soviet Union 2.9.

Most projections show world population nearly doubling by the year 2000. There is a ray of hope in a map accompanying one such projection that presents percentage increases geographically.

Europe will increase by only 15 percent, and, while that will make things a little tighter, there is no catastrophe in the offing. North America will increase her population by 64 percent and Oceania by 68 percent. Even here life will in all probability go on reasonably well, with the density still far from that already present in Europe. But Asia's population seems destined to increase by almost 90 percent, while Africa and Latin America swell more than 150 percent. So hope goes glimmering.

A man's home may not always be his castle, but his bedroom remains sacrosanct. Correctly or not, he considers what he does there his own private business. Thus it is doubtful that birth control will take hold in time to make a dent in current estimates. In the United States the increase may not be as large as was thought until recently, but in the undeveloped lands there is little encouragement in sight. ZPG is not here nor is it just around the corner. It will continue to come very slowly, perhaps following the lead of Europe. And so we must investigate the carrying capacity of Mother Earth.

For a territory the size of the United States five millions of people would be about right. . . . The human population of the entire world should be kept well under a hundred millions. . . . If the world were not so full of people, and most of them did not have to work so hard, there would be more time for them to get out and lie on the grass, and there would be more grass for them to lie on.

Don Marquis, "The Almost Perfect State"

CHAPTER 4

The Limits of Population

In 1960 President Eisenhower expressed what was still the "official" line on population control. He said, "I cannot imagine anything more emphatically a subject that is not a proper political or governmental activity or function or responsibility." Within a few years, however, he had changed his mind, as evidenced by an article in a national magazine.

In 1963 President Kennedy, a Roman Catholic, told a meeting of presidents of Central American countries: "If we do not stem this human tide now, we will all be inundated in an immense ocean of poverty." As we have said, however, it was President Johnson who first took the bull by the horns. Among his actions was the appointment of a study panel of experts, chaired by John D. Rockefeller III, an expert in the field of population.

In January 1969 this panel, the Committee on Population and Family Planning, made a report in which it urged the formation of a "population commission." On July 18 of that year President Nixon sent Congress the first formal message ever to come from the White House on population. In it Nixon pointed out that "many of our present social problems may be related to the fact

John D. Rockefeller, III, Chairman of the Commission on Population Growth.

that we have had only 50 years in which to accommodate the second hundred million Americans."

Within a week a bill setting up a Commission on Population Growth was introduced in the Senate. "Beefed up" in the House, the measure was signed by the President in March of 1970. Essentially the bill provides for a commission of twenty members, including a Democrat and a Republican from each house of Congress; provides for presidential appointment of members and officers; and outlines the commission's work:

1. To determine the probable course of U.S. population growth and internal migration.

2. To estimate the resources needed to deal with anticipated population growth.

3. To project the impact of population growth on federal and state governments.

4. To survey the effects of population growth on environmental pollution and the depletion of natural resources.

5. *To seek ways of achieving a population level commensurate with the ethical values and resources of the United States* [emphasis added].

Headed by Rockefeller, the commission is off and running. It is no secret that in point 5 it has a tiger by the tail, and already the ZPGers are doubting in print that the commission will meet the issue face on—just as the earlier blue-ribbon panel failed to call for curbs on population growth. It has taken our nation almost two centuries to take the threat of population growth seriously; it is unrealistic to expect that in a short time we will come up with the answers and machinery for population control. A preliminary report is due in one year, with a final report in two years.

Even if everyone were convinced that ZPG should become the new way of life, implementing such policy would not be easy. The problem is complicated—or perhaps simplified—by the fact that there is by no means unanimous agreement that we *have* reached what Representative John A. Blatnik (who added points 4 and 5 as amendments to the commission bill) and others call "optimum population" in the United States.

The population explosion, although it has only recently been discovered by many, is no new danger. For centuries a concerned few have worried and fretted over increasing numbers as a threat, predicting an approaching horror of, by, and for the numbers. These eventualities have not yet caught up with us. A billion—the population inhabiting the earth in Malthus's time—is a large number, but spaceship Earth is relatively large and a billion humans more or less rattled about on it. However, with 6 to 7 billion predicted by this century's end, Malthus's fears are beginning to have more meaning.

Like men swimming in a closed container partially filled with water, we have historically not really had any problem. But as the level of water—the human population—rises in the container, which remains the same size, the swimmers' heads rise ever closer to the roof. Just as only a certain volume of water will fit in a given container, there must be a limit to the number of humans the Earth will support. How many are too many? More sensibly, how many are enough?

Only a few brave crowd-lovers will deny that we have a human population problem. The present 3.5 billion (increasing at the lusty rate of nearly 200,000 per day) standing in line would reach 1.25 million miles—twenty-five times around the Equator, and then to the moon and back—a bread line of heroic proportions.

One alarmist has worked out the following horrible example of population explosion. Assume that the first humans reproduced to cause a modest population increase of 1 percent a year. In 5,300 years there would be 10^{23} humans crowding the Earth. This is 100,000,000,000,000,000,000,000, or 100 billion trillion human beings. Assuming an average weight of 100 pounds for each of them, they would weigh five billion trillion tons, approaching the weight of Earth itself! Since humans have a specific gravity of only 1, compared with about 5.2 for Earth, this swelling mass of humanity would have a volume 5.2 times that of Earth and thus form a covering thousands of miles thick. While the mind boggles, consider the fact that present population growth is not 1 percent but 2 percent a year, and that some experts see it increasing to 3 percent in the fairly near future.

Other mathematically inclined seers have produced charts showing that before long the population will indeed be exploding outward from Earth at the speed of light! These predictions are ridiculous, of course, since they produce biomass from nothing— a circumvention of Malthusian theory that not even the population explosion can justify. However, population *is* increasing alarmingly. Every year there are 70 million more humans among us— more than the population of Great Britain and Ireland, with Sweden thrown in for good measure. If this is not an "explosion," it will suffice until the real thing arrives.

The Malthusian Nightmare

The great concern over population pressure is no new scare. Benjamin Franklin in 1750 anticipated the people problem. French philosopher Antoine Nicholas de Condorcet saw a coming confrontation between increasing mouths to feed and a limited food supply. The English economist Sir William Petty also wrote of the problem, as did the German, J. P. Sussmilch. But it was England's Thomas Robert Malthus who wrote the classic preachment on overpopulation. In 1798 Malthus completed *An Essay on the Principle of Population as It Affects the Future Improvement of Society.* Because of the controversial nature of his subject, he published anonymously.

Franklin had sagely written that there was no bound to the proliferation of plants and animals except their own crowding and interference with one another for subsistence. As an example, he noted that if there were only one species it might take over the Earth. Malthus agreed with Franklin, although he correctly pointed out that man differs from the plants and irrational animals in that he has more control over his increasing numbers. Condorcet and Malthus's father had been optimistic over the future and thought that with birth control and other voluntary checks man would limit his population to reasonable numbers. But Malthus was not convinced that this was true. Population pressure, he claimed, was responsible for all sorts of moral abominations. As one who had taken holy orders, Malthus was especially concerned with the moral implications of population pressure; however, it is the mathematical and ecological aspects of his essay that have prevailed and for which his name has been most mentioned in the literature. Here is the extract of his Malthusian theory, with emphasis added to a key point:

The rate according to which the productions of the earth may be supposed to increase it will not be so easy to determine. Of this, however, we may be perfectly certain—that the ratio of their increase in a limited territory must be of a totally different nature from the ratio of the increase of population. *A thousand millions are just as easily doubled every twenty-five years by the power of population as a thousand. But the food to support the increase from the greater number will by no means be obtained with the same facility.* Man is necessarily confined in room. When acre has been added to acre till all the fertile land is occupied, the yearly increase of food must depend

Thomas Malthus, British cleric whose "Essay on the Principle of Population" warned of the population dilemma in 1800.
© *Radio Times Hulton Picture Library*

upon the melioration of the land already in possession. This is a fund which, from the nature of all soils, instead of increasing must be gradually diminishing. But population, could it be supplied with food, would go on with unexhausted vigor; and the increase of one period would furnish the power of a greater increase to the next, and this without any limit.

Malthus goes on with specific situations and uses numbers to make his theory more explicit. He starts with England itself:

The necessary effects of these two different rates of increase, when brought together, will be very striking. Let us call the population of this island eleven millions; and suppose the present produce equal to the easy support of such a number. In the first twenty-five years the population would be twenty-two millions, and the food being also doubled, the means of subsistence would be equal to this increase. In the next twenty-five years the population would be forty-four millions, and the means of subsistence only equal to the support of thirty-three millions. In the next period the population would be eighty-eight millions and the means of subsistence just equal to the support of half that number. And at the conclusion of the first century the population would be a hundred and seventy-six millions, and the means of subsistence only equal to the support of fifty-five millions, leaving a population of a hundred and twenty-one millions totally unprovided for.

The population of England today is only 55 million, not the 100 million plus Malthus envisaged, but still enough to demonstrate the agricultural lag in ability to feed an increasing number of stomachs. Much food is imported, of course. It is also true that there has been considerable emigration from England—not only a brain drain but a stomach drain as well. Malthus makes his most telling point in this regard:

Taking the whole earth instead of this island, emigration would of course be excluded; and, supposing the present population equal to a thousand millions, the human species would increase as the numbers 1, 2, 4, 8, 16, 32, 64, 128, 256, and the subsistence as 1, 2, 3, 4, 5, 6, 7, 8, 9. In two centuries the population would be to the means of subsistence as 256 to 9; in three centuries, as 4096 to 13; and in two thousand years the difference would be almost incalculable.

Fortunately, two centuries will produce only 6 or 7 billion people and not 256 billion. Malthus intelligently said that such incalculable numbers of population would not come about. Food would be the ultimate check, but he saw two other kinds of checks, which he stated had been operating to limit populations before famines took place. These were "preventive checks," peculiar to man; and "positive checks," operating on all living things. In man, preventive checks voluntarily limit the size of families. Malthus deplored some of these as immoral. Positive checks, affecting men, animals, and plants, include the "interferences" Franklin mentioned, disease, natural catastrophes, and so on. Man makes war against other men; some animals kill off competitors. These, too, are positive checks.

Although the twenty-five-year doublings of population Malthus feared have not taken place on a global scale as yet, it is interesting that the operation of his magic number *is* fast approaching. Best present estimates call for a doubling of world population in about the next thirty-five years, and if something does not check the increase by then, the next doubling may occur in even less time.

Immortal Billions

Complicating the picture is the probability of further increases in longevity. With organ transplants and the implanting of artificial organs, there may be more people, living for longer periods of time. If the wild-eyed schemes of the "body-freezers" come to pass, there may be more billions in our future than anyone feared. Quoting from Robert C. Ettinger's book *The Prospect of Immortality:*

If we consider the whole world, with a base population of, say, four billion, then the frozen population would increase by four billion every thirty years. If it takes 300 years for civilization to reach the immortality level, there would then be some forty billion people to revive and relocate. . . .

Ettinger's idea is that after "immortality" no one will die. Some have carried this idea to more ridiculous extremes and propose reconstructing *all those who ever lived*, by means of some sort of advanced "genetic engineering," using scraps of cellular material from long-dead corpses!

Ettinger charitably says, "There is ample room on our planet for forty billion people," forgetting how many other billions of *living* persons there may be on earth by that time. Fortunately the "freezer age" did not start in 1964 as he envisioned, and perhaps will not start at all.

The Neo-Malthusians

There is a tendency to ridicule Malthus as having been short-sighted about the probability of increased food production. He was not; in fact, he was aware that the animals man ate could multiply just as man could and that "sheep unrestrained could cover the earth in 70 years."

Malthus foresaw food production increasing in arithmetic ratio from 1 to 9 in two centuries; it is doing just about this well. But, as we shall see in future chapters, this is only the beginning. Malthus's gloomy example foretold 256 billion of us by the year 2000. If this fantastic increase had taken place so quickly we obviously could not have fed such numbers. Yet today there are estimates by experts that as many as 157 billion could be fed at some time in the future. One Russian economist sees far more humans than that in the offing, and the English scientist Fremlin admitted to the possibility of *billions* of billions of humans kept alive in a futuristic hell-on-earth not much more pleasant than the Black Hole of Calcutta. This would require using such science-fiction techniques as reflecting more sunlight onto Earth from space mirrors, and the like.

This, it might be asked, is living? If Malthus is right, we *must* hold population down to food supply. Even if he is wrong, why subject mankind to the jammed-up existence amid the numbers that the food supply could be made to support?

Preston Cloud, geologist at the University of California, Santa Barbara, in 1970 told the American Association for the Advancement of Science that 200 million in the United States and 3.5 billion on earth already exceed the optimum population. Although the National Academy of Sciences Committee on Resources and Man indicates that world food supplies might be increased ninefold and thus feed about 30 billion (a total that would be reached by 2075), Cloud sees 7 billion as the maximum number that might eventually be supported over the long term at a moderate level of affluence. Barry Commoner, director of the Center for the Biology of Natural Systems, Washington University, long the voice of ecology, also sees about twice the present population as a maximum.

Several other thinkers on population were quoted at the AAAS meeting:

Aristotle: "The best limit of the population of a state is the largest number which suffices for the purposes of life and can be taken in at a single view."

John Stuart Mill: "After a degree of density has been attained, sufficient to allow the principal benefits of combination of labour, all further increase tends in itself to mischief."

A Polynesian: "Families by Tikopia custom are made corresponding to orchards in the woods. If children are produced in plenty, then they go and steal because their orchards are few. So families in our land are not made large . . ."

Demographer Kingsley Davis in the *New York Times*, October 5, 1969, longs for the old days: "I happen to think this country would be better off with half the population. With our present technology and the population of the 1930s the country would be a paradise. As it is, it's getting to be like hell."

Pointing out that, as a class, the nonindustrial nations have been increasing since 1930 at twice the rate of the industrial nations, Davis said in *Scientific American:*

One is tempted to believe that the underdeveloped countries simply are repeating history: that they are in the same phase of rapid growth the West experienced when it began to industrialize and its death rates fell. If that is so, then sooner or later the developing areas will limit their population growth as the West did.

It is possible that this may prove to be true in the long run. But before we accept the comforting thought we should take a close look at the facts as they are.

Davis estimated that by the year 2000 India will have from 100 to 200 million migrants to cities, and a largest city of from 36 to 66 million inhabitants!

How Many Can We Feed?

Although it must seem bitter irony to all who are hungry, if not starving, many experts contend that while food is the ultimate check it is not food supply that holds down population. Distribution, politics, and other man-made factors are blamed, rather than the ability simply to produce food. There does seem to be truth in this view, strange as it may seem in light of all the programs to relieve the suffering of hunger. Further confusing the picture are those who claim we cannot feed present numbers, yet then proceed to say that if we do not check population we may soon have several times as many to feed! This would seem to indicate that we *can* feed more than present numbers.

K. Malin, a senior research worker in Moscow, made this statement in his paper "Food Resources of the Earth," U.N. World Population Conference, Belgrade, 1965:

. . . just by increasing the average per-acre yields of crops used for food to the level achieved in advanced countries, it is possible to increase the harvest from the present cultivated area of the world, and provide food for 9,000 million people. If all the vegetation on the earth's surface land were replaced by food and feed crops, at the present rate of photosynthesis it would be possible to obtain a sufficient quantity of food for 41,000 million to 58,000 million people. If the marine vegetation were included in the calculations the figure would be 290,000 million people. . . .

It 10 percent of the solar energy reaching the earth were used in the process of photosynthesis, with the vegetation period lasting not less than six months, it would be possible to obtain food for 10,000 people from one square kilometer, or for 100 people from one hectare. . . .

If we assume that the world's potential sown area is equal to 100 million square kilometers (10,000 million hectares), field farming on the earth's land surface may provide the food for a million million people. . . . If plant growing could be achieved in the world's ocean on the same scale as on the land our planet could provide the food for three to four million million people.

That last number, coincidentally, is just 1,000 times present population! It should be remembered that Communists deplore Malthusian theory and profess to favor a dynamically growing population, all with the blessings of abundance rather than all the good things hoarded for a select few.

Economist Colin Clark has estimated that all the arable land in the world would support 47 billion people at United States standards, and 157 billion at the Japanese level of subsistence.

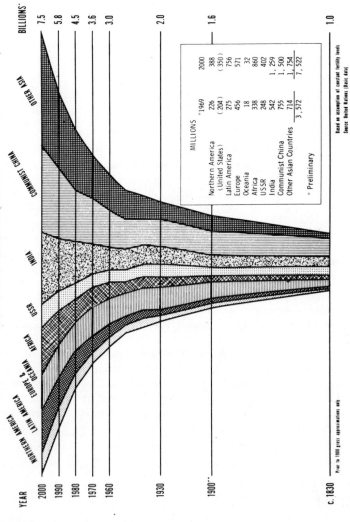

THE POPULATION BOMB
IN THE YEAR 2,000
WHERE THE PEOPLE WILL BE

MILLIONS	°1969	2000
Northern America	226	388
(United States)	(204)	(350)
Latin America	275	756
Europe	456	571
Oceania	18	32
Africa	338	860
USSR	248	402
India	542	1,259
Communist China	755	1,500
Other Asian Countries	714	1,754
	3,572	7,522

° Preliminary

Based on assumption of constant fertility levels
Source: United Nations (Basic data)

Reprinted with the permission of the Population Reference Bureau, Inc.

The Bigger the Better

Not all arguments are on the side of population control. Even Kingsley Davis, quoted as believing the United States is already twice its optimum size, earlier made this assessment of population growth and its prognosis in *Scientific American:*

We can see now that in all modern nations the long run trend is one of low mortality, a relatively modest rate of reproduction and slow population growth. This is an efficient demographic system that allows such countries, in spite of their "maturity," to continue to advance economically at an impressive speed.

Vocal among those who do not subscribe to the theory of cutting back population or drastically curbing its growth is Colin Clark. Citing the law of "increasing returns," he points out that it may actually be *detrimental* for a nation to remain small or become small. France voluntarily cut its size, to its regret, he says in *Population Growth and Land Use:*

It is a strange coincidence that in the year 1798, when Malthus was writing his book on the principles of population, and Jenner had just perfected vaccination, which was probably to do more than any other discovery to ensure population growth in Western Europe, Napoleon was successfully invading Egypt, and France, politically, came near to dominating the world. Malthus' own countrymen did not follow him, at any rate until much later, but the French did, and every Frenchman now is bitterly conscious that the decline of his country's influence in the world has been mainly due to its relatively lower rate of population growth. The English however have been slow in reaching a similar conclusion.

Kingsley Davis made a similar assessment for the French situation in *Scientific American:*

France, already crowded in the 18th century and in the van of intellectual radicalism and sophistication, was likely to have a low threshold for the adoption of abortion and contraception. The death rate, however, remained comparatively high because France did not keep pace with her more rapidly industrializing neighbors.

Clark cites an early writer on increasing returns, the Arab Ibn-Khaldun, who in the fourteenth century wrote:

The individual cannot satisfy his wants independently but must co-operate with his fellow men; the foodstuff is not produced by one's efforts nor does each one produce his own consumption; in its production co-operate six or ten, blacksmith, carpenter, laborer, etc. Now when all these co-operate, they produce together a quantity of foodstuffs by far exceeding their wants.

When civilization reaches the state of excesses and luxury with its accompanying vices, limits are automatically set on population. There happen then devastating famines. Famines are not the result of the land's incapacity to cope with the increasing demand but are the result of the political chaos and physical oppression which invade the state in its decline.

And this was written four centuries before Malthus.

Clark also mentions a number of other economists holding similar views. The notion of high population density as economically advantageous was analyzed by Sir William Petty in relation to the success of the Dutch, jammed into a tiny country but capable of standing up to and defeating major powers like England and France. More recently, Allyn Young has argued for increased population as an aid to industrialization, and suggested that England should have a population of 100 million, about double its present size.

Everett Hagen speaking at the International Association for Research on Income and Wealth in 1953 stated that densely populated countries need less capital per capita per unit of production than do sparse areas. He also claimed rapid population increase absolves a nation for its errors in planning.

Clark makes this point in *Population Growth and Land Use*:

Building therefore on this idea, originally developed by Malthus himself, we now reach a conclusion which is, in effect, a converse of Malthus's own original proposition, namely that, in a great many times and places, population is undesirably low, and may be increasing at a very low rate. The time comes, of course, when population growth does threaten to overtake the "means of subsistence," as they are understood in that time and place; and then the consequence is that population growth itself provides the necessary stimulus, inducing the community to change its existing methods of producing or obtaining food for more productive methods, which will enable it to support a larger population.

When England felt the need of calling for a special census of birth statistics in 1938, the Honorable Sir Alan Patrick Herbert brought down the House of Commons in 1938 by putting his criticism of a birth statistics bill into verse:

> They pulled down all the houses where the children used to
> crowd,
> And built expensive blocks of flats where children weren't
> allowed;
> And then when father got a job there wasn't anywhere to dwell,
> And the Minister still wonders why the population fell.
>
> Great science labored nobly to increase the people's joys,
> But every new invention seemed to add another noise;
> One was always on the telephone or answering the bell,
> And everybody wondered why the population fell.

The sad fate of their poor cousins across the water in Ireland might have been in the minds of Englishmen who favored continuing growth.

In a nation that has historically enjoyed, or at least experienced, population growth, what is the result of a reduction or the total elimination of growth? Ireland provides a case history. Its population was 8.2 million in 1841, but as a result of the potato famine and subsequent mass emigration, by 1901 the population had dropped to only 4.5 million. Presently it is only 2.9 million, although population has been increasing steadily since 1961.

Irish per capita income for 1969 was $910, compared with from $1,690 to $2,500 for the rest of northern Europe, statistics that do not speak well for the economic advantages of small population.

Japan is sometimes cited as an example of a nation that demonstrated it could reduce its population and prosper. However, while the Japanese have reduced their growth rate, it is still as

high as that of the United States. And the Japanese, who have
a density of population of about 800 per square mile (compared
with a little over 100 per square mile for Ireland), have one of the
most developed, literate, and prospering nations.

Clark calls Alfred Sauvy the leading exponent of the theory of
increasing returns, and Sauvy, a noted economist respected all
over the world, argues against curbing population. "If population
limitation were the key to economic progress," he said at the
1954 World Population Conference, "France would be the richest
country in the world for she has practiced it longest."

Ironically, Sauvy in 1939 analyzed the French budget and
found only 20 percent of it geared to population, the remaining
80 percent necessary regardless of the number of people. War
came in 1939 and France was short of budget, manpower, weapons, and other things needed to fight against a Hitler. In summing
up, Sauvy wrote in his book *General Theory of Population:* "The
historian cannot show us any example of population stagnation or
decline whose results have been happy."

Darwin Among the Antinatalists

In 1952, Charles Galton Darwin, grandson of the Darwin of
evolution fame and grandnephew of Sir Francis Galton, the
eugenicist, published a book called *The Next Million Years.* The
attention Darwin gave to population—even when there were only
2.5 billion people on Earth, is evidence of long concern by some
over the problem.

Claiming to believe that "the prospect of owning a motor-car
is sufficient bribe to sterilize most people," Darwin nevertheless
was convinced of the inevitability of further population increase
and even the necessity of it. If a nation shrinks its own size while
its neighbors are growing, does it not put itself in a disadvanta-
geous position?

The Polynesians are notable for their population-curbing tendencies. In *The Next Million Years* Darwin has some interesting comments on these island people:

Through insufficient knowledge I can only cite this example of the Polynesians very tentatively, but it does seem to show that a race adapted to limiting its population cannot compete against others which have not been similarly adapted.

It was no consolation to Darwin that some countries seemed to have succeeded in holding down population. Such phenomena were anomalies rather than accurate guideposts:

Any country which limits its population becomes thereby less numerous than one which refuses to do so, and so the first will be sooner or later crowded out of existence by the second. And again, the stationary population is avoiding the full blast of natural competition, and, following a universal biological law, it will gradually degenerate. It is impossible to believe that a degenerating small population can survive in the long run in a strongly competitive world, or that it can have the force to compel the rest of the world to degenerate with it.

Even the greatest efforts of international goodwill were given no hope of success by Darwin, as he expanded his argument to show the hopelessness of the situation:

Since the aim of the policy is to retain world-wide prosperity, every single country would be faced with the problem of taking care of its own limitation, and, as has been seen, this would not come about spontaneously. Even if a government could devise an effective method, it would be an odious task for the rulers to have to enforce it, and there can be no doubt they would often evade doing so. . . . It is clear from all this that the world policy would need to be supported by international sanctions, and the only ultimate sanction must be war. . . .

More recently, in *The Silent Explosion*, Philip Appleman writes of the same concern:

. . . The Russians are well past the 230 million mark; the Chinese have shot past 730 million. Both nations are still growing rapidly. In view of recent experience, totalitarian countries with high-birth policies cannot help but raise suspicions. Many of us remember all too vividly the high-birth policies of Hitler, Mussolini, and the Japanese—and the eventual call for *Lebensraum*.

Darwin has another concern about population control that goes even deeper, a fear that the loss of the "creative minority" was a contributing factor in the decline of past civilizations. Stated simply, his belief is that the more people born the more statistical chance there is for bright ones.

This is an argument that can be taken either way, however. Some observations with animals suggest that the buildup of population can lead to a weakening of the gene pool. If conditions are too good, most individuals survive and the population is hurt genetically. Interestingly, S. C. Reed has pointed out that an average past civilization lasted about 800 years, which equates to about thirty-one generations. Even a small decline in mental ability might eventually result in the collapse of a civilization.

Referring to studies showing that people in England and America are losing their intelligence at the rate of 1 percent to 2 percent per generation, Karl Sax concludes in *Standing Room Only*: "Certainly, in a society with equal opportunities for all, the higher birth rates of the lowest socio-economic classes would be dysgenic and could lead to a decline in the average intelligence of the population." This of course argues against Darwin and for population control as a means of maintaining intelligence levels.

In his book, Darwin makes an interesting comment that touches discouragingly on the concept of the "quality of life" so much mentioned in population control schemes:

The really wonderful thing about the last century has been that exciting improvements of condition have been happening at frequent intervals for about six generations. And even so, it is not very evident that those living in the present conditions of enhanced prosperity are any *happier* than the people described by Dickens.

Darwin points out the practical difficulty of conscious action on the part of present generations to aid those who will follow us in the future, asking: "Am I likely to refrain from putting coal on the fire on a cold evening by the thought that it may make one of my fourteenth descendants suffer for it?"

He concludes that population pressure will continue to be the central feature of history, and that there will always be a *starving margin* of humanity: "Whatever food the efforts of mankind may produce, there will always be exactly the right number of people to eat it."

ZPG–U.S.A.

As we have already seen, there are well-meaning groups crusading across the United States today urging drastic steps and even coercion if necessary, to achieve Zero Population Growth. A hundred years ago the population of the country was about 50 million. There were surely those at the time who thought that was far too many. But can it be proved that the quality of life today is less than that of a century past? And which 150 million of us would be willing to depart so that the 50 million left could be four times as happy? If 2 million new Americans each year pose a threat, what of the 250,000 immigrants annually admitted to our country? Should they be excluded, or might they not think the United States is still a pretty good place even with all its population?

Ansley Coale gave some thoughtful arguments on population increase in the United States in his presidential address to the Population Association of America in April 1968:

> Even if our population should rise to a billion [five times what it is now!] its average density would not be very high by European standards. It seems to me we must attack the problems of pollution, urban deterioration, juvenile delinquency and the like directly, and if sensible programs are evolved, continued population growth in the order of one percent annually would not make the programs tangibly less effective.

This seems to make sense. An increase of 100 percent over half a century is impressive, but how much do we notice 1 percent a year? Actually, the present population increase of only 0.8 percent is remarkably close to a perfect balance.

An argument in a recent editorial by Rufus E. Miles in *Population Bulletin*, February 1970, against "growthmania" uses the example of a father who as a boy enjoyed Yosemite but today is appalled by the "traffic jam within the park—40,000 people inhaling each other's fumes instead of breathing pure air and drawing inspiration from the grandeur of the cliffs and waterfalls." Here is a specious argument, as a little thought will show. Population has gone up only about 30 percent in the last generation, thus if population alone accounts for the present jam in Yosemite there would have been about 30,000 on hand at the earlier date! Such reasoning implies that its author resents the fact that increasing affluence makes it possible for more people to enjoy our parks.

Quoting Wordsworth's line on London: "Earth has not anything to show more fair," Colin Clark, in *Population Growth and Land Use*, has some misgivings but feels that even with larger populations:

> . . . our descendants will be able to recreate the beauty for which man hungers, without re-creating the crowded tenements, when town planners, economists and politicians have done what it is their duty to do, namely to enable people to live in moderately sized cities, with near access to unspoiled countryside.

Ansley Coale brings forward other arguments:

> A stationary population with an expectation of life of 70 years would have as many people over 60 as under 15. The distribution would be essentially vertical up to age 50 or 55. The median age would be about 37 years.
> A society with such an age structure would not be likely to be receptive to change and indeed would have a strong tendency towards nostalgia and conservatism. A French writer has characterized a stationary population as "a population of old people ruminating over old ideas in old houses." As Myrdal pointed out years ago, in a stationary population there is no longer the consonance that there is in a grow-

ing population between the pyramid of responsibility and the age pyramid.

However, Lincoln H. Day, associate professor of Public Health and Sociology at Yale University, says a median age of thirty-seven rather than today's twenty-seven would not produce an undesirable "society of greybeards in wheelchairs":

The current preference for youth and rapid change may itself be a reflection of our own period of unrepressed numerical and technological expansion. The assumption that rapid change is invariably a desirable condition of human life may well yield to a greater appreciation of the value of stability and continuity with the past.

What effect ZPG would have on youth's status is difficult to foresee, for it is also pointed out that while there would be less demand for the services of the young, there would also be fewer young to fill that demand.

Business writers echo the long-prevalent belief that a declining growth rate in the GNP brought about by slower population growth would increase the problems of employment and income redistribution. Yet a poll of the chief executives of the five hundred largest American corporations showed almost 80 percent favoring some kind of curb on further population growth. While it appears that with a stable population the economy would grow at only 3 percent a year instead of the present 4 percent, it is pointed out that the standard of living would nevertheless rise. The market would be smaller, but it would also be richer for business. And with smaller families, per capita income would be higher, thus giving each more of the material blessings.

To achieve Zero Population Growth in the United States would require about 2 children per family; actually, 2.1 is stated as the exact replacement rate. Just how this is to be achieved equitably may require Solomon's wisdom, if not his sword. Perhaps it may not be necessary.

When Malthus wrote his essay, the population of the United States was about 4 million. In less than two centuries it has climbed to almost 210 million, a more than fiftyfold increase. This is hardly a fair set of statistics, of course, for the population in the days of our first census was sparse indeed by any standards. A century later it had grown to 62 million, an increase of more than fifteen times. The last eighty years has seen it increase another three and one-half times or so.

Despite all the alarmed cries about population and the people explosion in our country, the facts are, as we have said, that our growth rate is at an all-time low. In 1968 the birthrate had dipped to 17.5, lowest in our history. In 1969 it increased slightly to 17.7, the first increase in more than ten years. Recent birthrates have been even lower than those of the depression years. Not long ago the Census Bureau was estimating a maximum of 361 million Americans by 2000. Now that estimate has been lowered to 320 million. And it is possible that there may not be even the 300 million once considered inevitable by then. The minimum estimate is only 261 million.

The Population "Crash"

We hear much of "togetherness," and within bounds such sociability is doubtless well and good. But there seem to be limits to how much human society we can stand. This is the basis for the "stress" theory enjoying much present popularity in explaining the strange behavior of the lemmings, hares, and some dense populations of mice, and possibly man's exploding numbers.

In the jargon of the day, the population problem is often referred to as the "crunch." The accepted term in the lexicon of science is "crash," although biologist René Dubos prefers "avalanche." With one eye on the population explosion, many scientists are keeping the other on the crashes that sometimes occur in other species—algae, for example, cultures of bacteria, the famous lemmings of Scandinavia, the less well-known hares of North America, and more recently the "induced crashes" in populations of rats through laboratory experiments with overcrowding.

There is much evidence for a population regulation system in animals, perhaps genetic in nature. Biologists tell us, for example, that where conditions are not disturbed, birds and other creatures apparently hold their numbers within very close limits. While it is true that over geological time nearly all species have become extinct, those that now exist seem to vary in number only by "ripples" and not "waves" over relatively long periods of time, say up to a century.

As early as Charles Darwin's time it was pointed out that there are relatively few numbers in each species, indicating some sort of control mechanism to hold them in check. Why don't some species take over and multiply to the detriment of others? Some biologists see a delicate "genetic feedback" system in nature: When predators begin to multiply and threaten to wipe out a plant or animal species, resistant types dominate, thus reducing the population of predators and slowly bringing the plant population back to its former level.

Man has upset the delicate natural balance, called "homeostasis," by introducing new species into certain areas. The rabbits that took over Australia are an example. Within twenty years these invaders abounded by the billions and were denuding the countryside. It was necessary for man to introduce yet another alien species, the virus myxomatosis, which quickly killed off the rabbits. In the first epidemic some 98 percent of the rabbits died. But by the sixth virus epidemic only 29 percent fatalities were incurred. Eventually a balance was reached between rabbits, virus, and the rest of the environment. This "climax ecology," or stable balance, will prevail until the next upset.

Beyond the homeostasis of nature, ecologists propose that social organization within a species is also a strong factor in maintaining populations within limits. The concept of "territoriality," popularized by author Robert Ardrey, plays a role here. In 1920, biologist Eliot Howard reported that female birds were cold to advances of all males except those with property. While this gold digger-like quality in the feathered species is a difficult concept to accept, it is the basis for the territorial theories held today. The bobwhite is cited as an example of a species that holds its numbers far below its powers of reproduction and the availability of food through psychological checks. The muskrat, too, is given as such an example, and there are others.

C. M. Breder, Jr., director of the New York Aquarium, in 1932 conducted an experiment with guppies that was claimed to challenge Malthusian theory and establish the principle of territoriality. Into one tank Breder put fifty guppies, in a distribution not to be found in nature—approximately equal numbers of adult males, adult females, and juvenile guppies. Into a second tank went one lone female, whose eggs had been fertilized. Six months later, both tanks contained three males and six females, a ratio found in natural guppy populations.

The point allegedly proved was that in completely different situations the "territorial imperative" had operated—not a shortage of food or some other necessity, but a built-in population governor to which the guppies responded and did away with the surplus. Physiological and behavioral factors supposedly resulted in the 2-to-1 female to male ratio in both tanks. In 1958, guppy experiments by R. P. Silliman and J. S. Gutsell showed similar results.

Much has been made of the strange behavior of the lemmings in Scandinavian countries. On a cycle from three to five years, these rodents migrate to the sea in mass suicide. (In North America the snowshoe hare exhibits similar behavior, but has not had as good a press.) Apparently it is not disease that does the animals in, or even food shortage but, as is thought by some biologists, a stress factor. Although degeneration of the liver, a shortage of blood sugar, and minor internal hemorrhages are sometimes found, the most striking thing is the physiological and psychological exhaustion evident. Behavior ranges from torpor to frenzied convulsions.

The stress is thought to come from high-density population, causing many young lemmings, increasing competition, and great numbers of strangers in the population. The result, in the theorists' view, is total social disorganization and mass insanity.

Studies of "population density and social pathology" with rats living in dense populations in the laboratory showed many females unable to carry pregnancy to full term, or, if they did, to die giving birth in most cases. Those that did give birth made poor mothers. Males exhibited deviant behavior, including cannibalism, homosexuality, frenzied overactivity, or withdrawal to the point of eating and drinking only when the other rats were asleep. "Pathological togetherness" was found to disrupt courtship, nest-building, and the nursing of young. Infant mortality was as high as 96 percent.

Biologist Paul Errington finds it ironic that man cannot do better than the lower animals in at least seeing the menace in irresponsible population increase. Errington said in *The Yale Review*, March 1962. "I confidently expect the troublous aspects of our population situation to be compounded the higher our numbers go, until the laws of life absolutely put a stop to further increase."

Whether or not one of those laws will result in a great human population crash remains to be seen, but considerable increase in our numbers seems inevitable. And while the debate about population goes on we must continue to feed those numbers. From a practical and immediate standpoint, the population problem boils down to one of food supply.

Part II.

The Food Problem

And God said, Let there be light: and there was light . . .
Genesis 1:3
And God said, Let the earth bring forth grass . . .
Genesis 1:11

CHAPTER 5

The Food Chain

The energy used for food comes not from Earth itself but from the sun, that hot star some 93 million miles away. Were its light to go out, man's would, too, unless he learned to exploit atomic or nuclear energy in a fashion analogous to the sun's light and heat. The sun consists of a ball of hydrogen continuously being converted into helium, plus a leftover in the form of radiant energy. We owe our lives and our all to this by-product energy, which the sun beams to us across the eight-minute gap.

Although sunbeams can burn our skin, we generally consider them as the poets do, soft and zephyrlike. In fact, they are highly energetic. While earth receives only a tiny fraction of the total solar energy, this pittance amounts to a constant 170 trillion kilowatts of power. A single square centimeter, the scientist's favorite area measurement, receives slightly less than two calories of solar energy each minute. One calorie raises the temperature of one cubic centimeter of water one degree Centigrade and thus is not a powerhouse. But in a square inch there are more than six square centimeters and when we calculate something the size of an average house roof we find that it receives enough energy

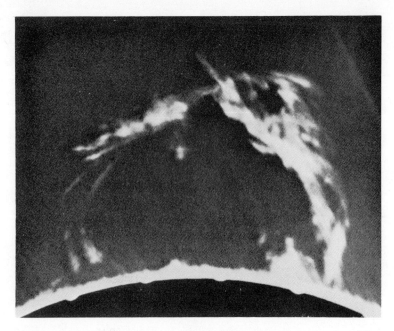

All our food energy comes originally from the sun, some 93 million miles away.
Solar Energy Society

on a sunny day to match that contained in the gas tank of the family automobile.⁷

On a global basis man consumes something like 4.5 billion kilowatts of power in his mechanical contrivances. Coincidentally, at the same time he consumes about an equivalent amount in food energy. The reason we have shifted from burning wood for power production is that if we burned *all* the vegetation on earth as fuel it would just about take care of our power needs—and leave us starving to death.

At a reasonable estimate of 1.5 calories per square centimeter per minute, the United States receives a whopping total of about 8 million trillion calories of solar energy each year. This would allow 3,000 kilocalories of food per day for each of 8 *trillion* human beings. At a kilowatt of solar energy per square meter of land and eight hours of sunlight a day, we get a rough and ready total of enough calories to feed two or three humans per square meter of land surface—people packed just about shoulder to shoulder. Working this out globally comes to so many trillions as to be ludicrous, so it is a relief to know that practical considerations dictate that even the most productive areas of earth support only one human being per thirty square meters, a fertile garden plot some seventeen feet on a side. A barren plot would be such a poor provider that humans subsisting on it would be out of sight of each other, as ranchers in the Southwest know from the small numbers of cattle they can run on a section of such land.

Incoming solar energy could support these fantastic numbers of people only if it were possible to convert sunbeams into food energy directly with no efficiency loss in the process. Unfortunately, or perhaps fortunately for those of us who enjoy our food, man is not a green plant, the only living thing that uses the process of photosynthesis to feed itself.

Green plants, also known as "independent" plants, represent the bulk of plant life. They are the only living things that need no energy but sunlight to exist, although of course they do require proper soil, moisture, gases, and minerals. Until man learns how to produce carbohydrates synthetically (and he is still some distance from a practical solution at this date), plant life soaking up sunshine is our only source of food, with one minor exception. We do make some use of the "sarcophytes," or feeders on decomposing matter. These include fungi like mushrooms and yeast, but while experiments indicate that we can grow yeast on petroleum, remember that petroleum itself is the product of decomposed matter originally created by the sun.

It is conceivable that we might use radiant energy other than that from the sun to fuel the photosynthetic process. At present some species of flowers and plants are being grown to a minimal extent in artificial light. Only if we are successful in harnessing some tremendous energy source—by the fusion of heavy water isotopes, for example—would farming by lamplight be a potential food source for the world. And fusion power seems farther down the scientific and technological pike than is the synthesis of food.

Let's look at the process of photosynthesis that makes Earth unique among the planets of the solar system, and perhaps in the universe.

Photosynthesis

Photosynthesis, a chemical reaction, is spelled out in the following basic formula:

$$CO_2 + H_2O + chlorophyll + light = H_2CO + O_2 + chlorophyll$$

CO_2 is carbon dioxide, present in the atmosphere in relatively small quantity. H_2O is water, of course. The green plant provides chlorophyll as the catalyst or process initiator. Light comes from the sun. On the right-hand side of the equation is H_2CO, the organic matter that we know more familiarly as fuel, or food. Carbohydrate is a more common term. Carbon is the stuff of life, a constituent of so-called organic materials. Life, it has been said with tongue in cheek, is one of the more interesting properties of carbon. Indeed, without carbohydrates there would be no life.

Chlorophyll, the "green magic" of hucksters who for a time put it into everything from chewing gum to toilet paper, performs real chemical magic in photosynthesis. Water and carbon dioxide, from which carbohydrates come, absorb light only in the short ultraviolet and long infrared wavelengths. They are transparent in visible sunlight. Here is where chlorophyll steps in as a catalyst to make the process work, for the chlorophyll of living plants absorbs visible sunlight, up to 6,800 "angstroms" (red light), and becomes "activated." More importantly, it passes on energy to the water, which in turn releases a hydrogen atom from each molecule for reaction with carbon dioxide to produce carbohydrates. Three "photons" (the basic "packet" of light energy) of red light, or two of blue light, should produce one molecule of carbohydrate H_2CO. This is a theoretical figure, however, and on the average only one carbohydrate molecule is formed for each eight photons absorbed.

In the laboratory, under optimum conditions, researchers have reported efficiencies of conversion for photosynthesis of about 30 percent. However, an acre of agricultural land in the temperate zones produces only two or three tons of dry carbohydrates instead of the theoretical potential of 500 times that much. Thus the average efficiency of photosynthesis in the field is only about 0.2 percent instead of the 30 percent achieved in the laboratory. There are a number of reasons for this, including the fact that there is something like 0.03 percent of carbon dioxide in the atmosphere, instead of the 3 percent used in the laboratory experiments; temperatures are not always ideal; the growing season does not last the whole year; and chlorophyll is not present uniformly over the surface of the farm. In theory, then, there is room for a five-hundredfold improvement in crop yield for a given land area.

Efficiency is a relative matter. Even operating at a conversion rate of a fraction of 1 percent, a green cell can produce up to thirty times its own volume of oxygen every hour. While food-stuffs are obviously not produced at that rate, the photosynthetic process each year transfers some 100 billion tons of elemental carbon from the inorganic form into the organic as carbohydrates!

The chlorophyll catalyst comes through the photosynthetic process unchanged, to be used again and again. The other product is oxygen, which purifies our atmosphere. Here is the elegant ecological balance, with plants not only providing us with food but cleaning up our atmosphere as well. Carbon dioxide disappears in the process, linking with water to form organic foodstuff. Were this one-way process to continue indefinitely, the trace amounts of carbon dioxide in the atmosphere would slowly vanish and plants would no longer produce carbohydrates. But the animals and men who consume plants for food put carbon dioxide back into the system as waste.

When we breathe we pollute the air—with carbon dioxide. So

Plants tilted to receive direct rays of sun for more growth.
Solar Energy Society

does combustion, the oxidation of vegetable matter to produce heat, ash, and carbon dioxide. Man has been dumping ever greater amounts of carbon dioxide into the atmosphere since his technology added the engine, a great consumer of organic fuel. It might seem that this would be a beneficial chemical change, since plants, with more carbon dioxide to work with, could then be more efficient in photosynthetic conversion. Over the ages, however, nature has geared the process to available amounts of the gas, and will take some time to adjust the delicate chemical processes to take advantage of the greater amounts of carbon dioxide.

This simple description of photosynthesis does not include many other important aspects of plant growth, including the need for minerals and soil and proper temperature. We will look at these factors in more detail in another chapter.

All Flesh Is Grass

The Bible, in Genesis 1:11, tells us: "And God said, Let the earth bring forth grass . . ." Grass had to come first, since it is the only living thing that needs no source of energy other than sunshine. Green plants are the primary source of food from which come the various secondary and tertiary food sources man uses to satisfy his sophisticated appetite. In spite of that sophistication, let us not forget that the basis is the green plant, of which the grasses are most important. In his chilling novel *No Blade of Grass*, English author John Christopher describes the brutal battle for survival when a mysterious virus wipes out *all* grasses, thus cutting off most of the food supply at its very beginning.

The 1970 corn blight in the United States brought Christopher's thesis into sharp focus. Isaiah was not only prophesying when he wrote that all flesh is grass, and would wither like grass, he was stating a profound ecological truth as well.

Botanists count some 350,000 different kinds of plants in the world today. Of these, about 250,000 are green plants; that is, they contain chlorophyll. Plants differ in some important respects from animals. They are fixed in position and they have the ability for almost unlimited growth. Animals gave up something when they acquired the power of locomotion and thus cut their direct ties to soil or water. They lost the power of unlimited growth, and they also lost the power of converting sunlight into food energy, making them dependent on green plants for food.

The flowering seed plants that feed the world represent the fifth and highest evolutionary level of plants, and perhaps billions of years of development. However, there are still representatives of the four preceding levels. *Procaryota*, the first stage of plant life, gave rise to blue-green algae and bacteria. Next came *Eucaryote*, known today in flagellate organisms classified either as algae or protozoa. These gave rise to eight phyla of aquatic plants. *Chlorophyta* came next, the first and most important single step in the conquering of land by plants. *Tracheophyta*, primitive vascular or veinous plants, were next. And finally came the seed plants, including the angiosperms, or flowering plants we cultivate for food. These are estimated to have appeared about 200 million years ago.

Only after plants were established, using solar energy to produce solid organic matter, did animals appear, since the latter feed on green plants.

Animals

In an age-old game, all objects are categorized as animal, vegetable, or mineral. The food chain is even simpler, and we drop the mineral category. Animals, the second and successive levels, are defined as any living things not plants, and while scientists profess to have difficulty in classifying some forms of life, most laymen identify animals as meat-producers.

There are still some single-celled life forms that are hard to classify as plant or animal and are in fact called "plantimals," since they seem animals yet get nourishment directly from the sun as do plants. Bacteria and molds developed mobility and retained the ability to synthesize all needed amino acids from the environment.

There are about three times as many species of animals as there are plants—close to one million of them, with new ones being discovered at the rate of 10,000 or so a year. These do not represent newly evolved species; it simply takes naturalists a while to find and classify all the animals there are in the world.

Evolutionists believe it all began with *Protozoa*, or "first animals." After that came *Protostomia*, or worms, allied to which are the crustaceans, mollusks, and insects. There are also the *Chordata*, or creatures that possess a spinal cord nervous system: the fishes, amphibians, reptiles, birds, and mammals. Man gets his food from a variety of families in the animal kingdom: mammals, birds, amphibians, fish, mollusks, and crustaceans.

The Living Sea

We have talked of photosynthetic production of carbohydrates on land. Similar production takes place in the sea; in fact, some writers estimate that the sea produces food energy at a rate equivalent to 45 billion kilowatts, compared with the 4.5 billion kilowatt equivalent required presently to feed our billions.

In many ways the oceans are ideal sites for the photosynthetic process. More than two-thirds of the Earth's surface is water, thus there is more than twice as much surface to trap sunshine. There is a hundred times as much carbon dioxide in the water as there is in an equal amount of air, and surely there is plenty of water to fuel the photosynthetic process. Not all writers on the subject of the sea's food potential are optimistic, however, and some claim that only a moderate further increase in catch is probable. We shall look more closely at this controversy in a later chapter.

The marine life cycle is more involved than that on land, with additional links in the so-called food chain. There are of course the primary sources, the independent sea plants that need only the energy of the sun for food. These phytoplankton, or vegetable plankton, are microscopic life forms that are fed on by increasingly larger animal life. First comes zooplankton, or animal plankton, some of them microscopic. There are also small fish that eat plant plankton. Next are fish that eat zooplankton, and then several levels of carnivores. At the top of the chain again is man.

Marine life may be divided into three groups: nekton, freely migrating swimming animals; plankton, the floating or drifting plants and animals; and benthos, plants or animals living at the bottom of the sea. Plants can live only in the photic, or light, zone, which extends downward about 300 feet, so there are far fewer benthic plants than animals. Bacteria also abound in the upper waters and in the deposits on the sea bottom.

As in the land food chain, carbon dioxide taken up in the photosynthetic process is later returned to the sea through life processes and also through death and decay. Although there is so much more carbon dioxide in the sea than in the air, the oceans produce no more carbohydrates per area exposed to sunlight than do land areas. There are "wet deserts" as well as dry deserts, and some of these nonproductive parts of the sea—identifiable by the blue color of the water, incidentally—yield as little as 0.1 gram of carbohydrates per day per square meter (a little more than a square yard). Average grassland, farming operations, and lakes and coastal waters produce ten to a hundred times this much. Intensive farming, rain forests, estuaries, coral reefs, and some springs may yield twice this much again. Highest reported yields, in experimental farming and in polluted water, reach twenty-five grams per meter, some 250 times that of wet and dry deserts.

Pyramids of Food

Green plants form the base of a food "pyramid." The next level consists of the herbivores, or plant eaters, of which there are a wide variety, from insects to ruminant animals (those with a series of stomachs, making it possible for them to convert forage to assimilable food), to man. Last are the carnivores or predators, which again include many types, from insects to animals to man.

This is a gross simplification of the food chain, and makes no mention of the fact that at different times organisms may feed on different portions of the chain, or on more than one at the same time. Some insects, for example, not only prey on man but eat the juice of plants, too. There are also fungi and bacteria in the food chain that feed on decomposed matter. These are important to the chain, although their importance is not as readily evident as the relationship between grass, beef cattle, and a steak dinner. The feedback between predator and prey, environmental factors, losses as heat and movement, and so on are glossed over in this skim treatment. But the main point should stand out—the apex of the pyramid is man, and he stays there because of the broad base several levels below.

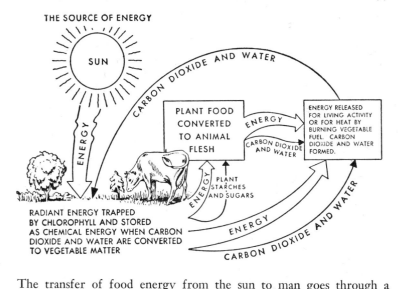

THE SOURCE OF ENERGY

SUN

CARBON DIOXIDE AND WATER

ENERGY

PLANT FOOD
CONVERTED
TO ANIMAL
FLESH

ENERGY

CARBON DIOXIDE
AND WATER

ENERGY RELEASED
FOR LIVING ACTIVITY
OR FOR HEAT BY
BURNING VEGETABLE
FUEL. CARBON
DIOXIDE AND WATER
FORMED.

ENERGY

PLANT
STARCHES
AND SUGARS

RADIANT ENERGY TRAPPED
BY CHLOROPHYLL AND STORED
AS CHEMICAL ENERGY WHEN CARBON
DIOXIDE AND WATER ARE CONVERTED
TO VEGETABLE MATTER

ENERGY

CARBON DIOXIDE AND WATER

The transfer of food energy from the sun to man goes through a
cycle in which carbon dioxide of the air is changed to plant fuel or
food and then to animal food. By burning or by life processes the
carbon dioxide is again released. It can then enter the cycle again
when green plants absorb more solar energy.
Reproduced by permission of Charles Scribner's Sons from The Sun, the
Sea, and Tomorrow *by Henry Chapin and F. G. Walton Smith. Copyright 1954 Charles Scribner's Sons*

We eat fruits and nuts and berries, green plants all. Some people have eaten plankton and algae in small amounts, along with
seaweed. Our daily bread is largely made of cereal grain, a green
plant. Many vegetables are eaten as well. Much of our diet is not
firsthand, however, but far along in the food chain. And each
step of that chain entails a great loss of efficiency in the conversion
process.

A steak is relished by most humans, but many cannot afford
such luxury in food intake because a pound of beef represents
about ten pounds of grain. Fish, advocated as a means of extending the food supply, is the end of the marine food chain, a chain
of many more links than the dry land chain, with each link repre-

senting a loss of 90 percent of the caloric value of the food, a so-called "law of tithes."

It has been estimated roughly that each pound of weight a man consumes as fish represents 1,000 or more pounds of plankton. Here is a final efficiency of only 0.1 percent. And the original photosynthetic process that produced the plankton from sunlight and chemical material was only about 0.2 percent efficient. So from sun energy to human food represents a loss of 499,000 parts in 500,000!

An "energy pyramid" worked out for Silver Springs, Florida, shows a production of 20,810 kilocalories per square meter per year by the plants. Only 8,833 kilocalories of this potential are passed on to the first carnivores. These carnivores make use of only 383 kilocalories of that amount, and pass on 67 to the top carnivores, who turn only 6 into useful biomass! Here is an efficiency through only four levels of the pyramid of only 6 parts in 20,810! Or 1 in 3,933 or 1/40 of 1 percent.

This is nature at her inefficient worst. Man has demonstrated that improvements can be made, and there are claims of feed-to-meat conversion ratios as high as one pound of meat for two pounds of feed in some cases, such as automated poultry raising and certain kinds of fish farming. Critics attack this kind of mathematics as omitting the fact that such gains occur at only selected portions of the growth of the animal, and otherwise exaggerating the case. However, they still beat 1 to 4,000!

There are many nonproducers in the food chain. Insects represent a great bulk of the biomass of the earth, but yield only minimal food benefits in most cases. There are noticeable exceptions, such as bees, which provide us with honey, and such fads as chocolate-covered ants sold as delicacies. But often hordes of grasshoppers, locusts, crickets, and other pests denude great areas of farmland, thus depriving us of the carefully nurtured food supply. Perhaps the answer is to fight fire with fire and eat these predators as food, although how many among us could subsist on locusts and honey as John the Baptist did is questionable.

Also, many animals are grown not for food but for wool, leather, to be kept as pets, and so on. But while pets are often fed table scraps, and some meat animals are fed garbage—a practice being discouraged in some areas because of hog cholera and other diseases—yielding valuable protein from what would otherwise have been waste, these hardly represent solutions to the problem, which is not simple; in fact, ecological systems and food chains are so complex that what looks like a proper approach in killing off a seeming pest can result in ecological chaos.

While there is room for improvement in the conversion of sun energy to food, the answers are seldom straightforward. For example, meat is often termed a "luxury" food, yet the animals that produce it often subsist on vegetation humans could not use for food. Meat animals also synthesize protein and other needed nutrients—for example, vitamins—not present in the grass or grain they eat. It is easy to talk of living on grains, but many people who are forced to do so suffer from malnutrition caused by lack of meat and meat products in the diet.

There is a fantastic amount of potential food energy in the sun, then. Sufficient calories beam down on us to support many more billions than anyone foresees populating the Earth in the next several centuries, but we may have to find more efficient ways of recovering those calories of energy. Much work already has been done in this direction, and many more possibilities abound. These will be discussed in succeeding chapters.

All I have learned about nutrition is this: If people are hungry, they need food. If they are ill-nourished, they need good food.

> Lord Boyd Orr
> First Director General
> of the United Nations Food
> and Agriculture Organization

CHAPTER 6

Nutrition

Frederick S. Hulse, in his book *The Human Species*, describes the eating habits of animals with remarkable economy of words:

In general animals exploit the fact that plants create food and return oxygen to the atmosphere. Larger animals kill and eat smaller ones, while microorganisms feed upon all sorts of larger creatures and are themselves the victims of virus infections. Many bacteria inhabiting the digestive tracts of bigger creatures assist them in digesting their food by enzymic activity.

Man's alimentary canal does do an efficient job—by means of mechanical and chemical actions and with the help of bacteria—in converting food into energy and the other requisites of life. Food is ground and chopped in the mouth, and digestion begins there. The stomach and intestines carry on the process, and blood extracts "fuel" to move our muscles and operate our brains. Waste products are rejected and eventually recycled in the over-all ecological system.

In general man requires daily three pounds of water, one and one-half pounds of food, and two pounds of oxygen to mix with food fuel for energy. We die first from oxygen starvation, second from lack of water, and last—and most prevalently—from starvation. ⸮

It has been pointed out that the world uses something like 4.5 billion kilowatts in the engines and motors necessary for our mechanized world, and coincidentally consumes about the same total "food power." We cannot subsist on wood or coal or gasoline or oil or natural gas—although experimental work indicates that such fuels can be used indirectly to provide food for man. We must have a special kind of fuel to function as living beings.

Webster defines food very succinctly: "1a: material containing or consisting of carbohydrates, fats, proteins, and supplementary substances (as minerals) used in the body of an organism to sustain growth, repair, and vital processes and to furnish energy." There is one other vital function of food: to permit man to reproduce, and thus to increase the need for food! It is this never-ending cycle that has led to our present problems.

In measuring the energy in food, scientists use heat as a standard, and gauge food value in calories or, more correctly, kilocalories. A kilocalorie of heat raises the temperature of a kilogram (2.2 pounds) of water one degree Centigrade. The caloric content of food is measured by its heat, when burned electrically in a special container. By carefully weighing the sample and just as carefully noting the amount of heat produced, nutritionists can very accurately find the caloric content of our various foods.

Heat is the basic form of energy. For comparison, a gallon of gasoline contains about 26,000 kilocalories of energy. To operate an average-sized car for a twenty-four-hour day would require about seventy-five gallons of gasoline. Because man is a "fractional-horsepower" machine, he needs only a fraction of this amount of fuel, and the equivalent of about one-tenth gallon of gasoline does the trick for most of the world's people. In fact, most of the world's population gets by on less than 2,600 kilocalories a day.

A standard, half-inch-thick slice of bread contains about sixty-four calories. Thus the forty slices in a twenty-inch loaf provide all the *caloric* intake a human needs. Add a jug of wine and some feminine companionship and the poet is blissfully happy. Bread is indeed the staff of life, but nutritionally we need something more than the carbohydrates found in our daily bread. We also need proteins, fats, vitamins, and traces of mineral elements.

The Minerals

Food may be broadly divided into two groups: inorganic and organic. Inorganic foods include water and mineral salts, which latter are also known as ash. While we don't normally consider it, water is present in most food, and makes up about 70 percent of the body. It is an important part of the diet, being an essential component of body cells, and also needed for ridding the body of wastes, cooling it, and so on. To use protein properly the body requires four times as much water by weight. Water does not yield energy or build or repair tissue, but it is nevertheless of vital importance to each cell and the body as a whole, as we have seen. The same is true of the minerals, even though they do not give us any energy or build tissue, either. Teeth and bones, for example, depend on minerals. Mineral requirements appear to be linked with those for vitamins, and also with glandular activity. Minerals function as catalysts, activators, regulators, and metabolizers. Those needed by humans include calcium, phosphorus, magnesium, sodium, potassium, manganese, iron, copper, cobalt, iodine, sulfur, zinc, aluminum, bromine, fluorine, and silicon.

Carbohydrates and Fats

In Chapter 5 we saw that plants produce carbohydrates from water and carbon dioxide. Among the carbohydrates are glucose, starch, sucrose, lactose, fructose, maltose, glycogen, dextrin, and cellulose. Carbohydrates would suffice if the human machine required only energy, as does the automobile engine, because carbohydrates are used by the body chiefly as sources of heat and energy.

Fat is another needed food. Technically, fats are "esters," or compounds of fatty acids with various alcohols. We need certain fats, and thus far three definite types have been identified: linoleic, linolenic, and arachidonic. These "lipids" are vital requisites of a proper diet. A hungry person "burns up" fat first, and a gram of fat gives up about nine calories, to only four for protein or carbohydrates. Fats comprise 20 to 40 percent of the diet in the developed countries, coming mostly from animals, and including meat, milk, and eggs. In undeveloped countries much less fat is consumed, and this fat, deriving largely from plants, includes soybeans, peanuts, olive oil, coconuts, sesame seed, and cottonseed. Avocados are particularly rich in fats.

Protein

Pointing out that man does not live by bread alone generally makes reference to the fact that we have spiritual needs as well. But, as we have already said, there is dietary truth in the statement as well. Since man's food needs are not just for heat and energy—which carbohydrates and fats provide in good quantity—but for growth and maintenance of his body, he needs other food components, in the form of protein. When inadequate amounts of calories are eaten, the body "lives off itself" by using up tissue material. If hunger persists until all spare fat and carbohydrate is consumed, the body begins to cannibalize functioning cells for protein to use as energy. Protein is a most important food, since it can provide heat and energy as well as body maintenance.

Living tissue is a complex array of physical and chemical processes and requires the constant addition of nitrogenous material for its proper maintenance. Protein molecules differ from those of carbohydrates. Carbohydrate structure is simple; protein molecules are giant molecules joined in linkages called "peptide chains." These twenty or so substances are more familiarly known as "amino acids," and man needs at least eight of them in his food to stay alive and well: isoleucine, leucine, lysine, methionine, phenylalanine, threonine, tryptophan, and valine. Five other amino acids are partially essential, and there are seven other amino acids present in the body, but apparently we can synthesize these from others provided in our diet.

These proteins grow tissue, make needed repairs in our cells, produce antibodies for disease fighting, and produce the enzymes, hormones, and hemoglobin we need to function properly. They also maintain the vital pH, or acid-alkaline chemical balance in our systems.

Plants, although they grow in the air, which is nearly 80 percent nitrogen, are unable to take in very much of that element. The best protein-producing plants are those whose roots play host to hordes of bacteria that pay for their keep by "fixing" nitrogen present in the soil surrounding them. Soybeans, excellent food plants, are about 35 percent protein. But meat is far better as a source of nitrogenous compounds, and is predominantly protein and very low in carbohydrates.

Animals function as processors and refiners, extracting protein from the low-protein plant food they consume and storing it up in their flesh for man to eat as steaks, roasts, bacon, kidneys, liver, and so on. So we operate our meat animals as living food factories, processing low-protein plants into high-protein meat products. We pay a price, of course, in loss of efficiency. Ten pounds of grain, representing 15,000 calories, yields only one pound of meat with 1,500 calories. But we must tithe in this manner to get the requisite amounts of animal proteins in our diet.

Other animal products are excellent foods. Milk, often called the perfect food, contains all the nutrients man needs, with the exception of iron. Butter and cheese are produced from milk, and all these by-products, as well as eggs, are most nutritious for man.

Typical Foods
(*with Protein Content and Cost per Pound*)

Cottonseed flour	55%	$ .05
Chick-peas	20	.06
Lysine	100	.07
Toasted soy protein	50	.11
Wheat flour	11	.11
Beans	22	.24
Fish protein concentrate	85	.25
Skim milk powder	36	.31
Dried fish	37	.36
Incaparina	28	.47
Cheese	25	1.11
Chicken	19	1.23
Beef	15	1.64
Pork	10	1.97
Eggs	11	2.04
Lamb	12	2.28

SOURCE: *Technology Review*, February 1970.

Vitamins

Casimir Funk coined the word "vitamin" about 1910, from *vita*, for life, and *amine*. Vitamins, organic compounds needed in addition to carbohydrates, proteins, and fats, act as "coenzymes" or other catalytic agents, and a dozen or more have been identified as vital to good health. There are two types of vitamins: those soluble in fats and those soluble in water.

Fat-soluble vitamins include the well-known vitamin A, important for health generally and good vision in particular. There are also vitamin D, the "sunshine vitamin"; vitamin E, which is important in the reproductive processes; and vitamin K.

The water-soluble vitamins consist of various B vitamins, including thiamine, riboflavin, nicotinic acid, B_6, pantothenic acid, folic acid, B_{12}, and vitamin C. Even though our vitamin requirements are listed in milligrams, or even micrograms (thousandths or millionths of grams), these "accessory food factors" are of vital importance.

Hungry World

All the many varieties of animal life are made of proteins containing about twenty amino acids. These varieties can themselves manufacture only about half these needed components of life. This is the price of evolution. To move about as free agents, animals had to learn to feed on plants or the bodies of other animals. Those that developed muscular and nervous systems did this better, and man, the most developed in these regards, prospered most in his ability to draw on other life for his food. This being true, it is strange that these days, when nutritional science has reached a high stage of sophistication, it sometimes seems almost impossible to get a proper diet, even with all our modern food-making and supplementing techniques. And here we are speaking, not of hunger, but of malnutrition.

Hunger and malnutrition are different miseries. Writing in *Scientific American*, February 1967, N. W. Pirie says: "Until the present century some people have been hungry all the time and all people have been hungry some of the time." Long before hunger began to wane, however, malnutrition had begun to trouble man, even the plentifully fed. In seventeenth-century England, for example, twenty-two of thirty-two royal children, from James to Anne, died before reaching age twenty-one. It is unlikely that the poor fared even this well. Two centuries later scurvy is said to have killed 10,000 or so forty-niners in California. As Pirie explains it:

Malnutrition appears when the food eaten is supplying enough energy, or even too much, but is deficient in some components of a satisfactory diet. Its presence continually and on a large scale is a technical triumph of which primitive man was incapable because he lacked the skill to process the food he gathered in a manner that would remove some of the essential components but leave it palatable and pleasing in appearance. . . .

The right policy is not to try to go back to nature and eat crude

During surveys of the nutritional status of the population of Central American countries it was not only proved that malnutrition is a widespread scourge, but that its origin is a complicated one: the poverty, the scarcity of food available, intermingled with traditional taboos, produces a very high infant mortality rate and stunted growth and development of the victims of malnutrition.

WHO photo, issued by FAO

foods but widespread knowledge of the principles of nutrition and enough good sense to use our technical skill prudently.

Nutrition is a relatively new field. A century ago Professor Lyon Playfair of the Department of Chemistry at the University of Edinburgh (one of those who tried to find the cause of the potato blight in Ireland), made the first scientific analyses of protein uptake in humans. He published reports indicating that two ounces of protein a day was required by an adult for survival. Perhaps not coincidentally, this was the exact amount the university hospital provided for patients on subsistence diets.

Playfair conceded that this was the minimum protein requirement, of course. Three decades later a German researcher found that the average German working man consumed four ounces of protein daily. However, this was later questioned as an ideal amount following a U.S. scientist's studies of his own rheumatic pains: a low-protein diet not only eased his aches but also improved his health. Subsequent field studies with groups of soldiers on low-protein diets were said to indicate that the men enjoyed better health than those fed large amounts of meat.

The old saying about one man's meat being another's poison is thus borne out nutritionally. Rather than prescribe fixed amounts of carbohydrates, fats, proteins, and vitamins across the board for everyone, the trend now is to study individuals and prescribe for them to suit their apparent genetic makeup and needs. There are good reasons for this approach, as seen in the following example.

England made early scientific strides in the battle against malnutrition when it more or less eliminated rickets, a bone disease brought on by a lack of vitamin D. By fortifying baby food with additional amounts of vitamin D concentrates, the government wiped out the disease but found that a few children began to die of kidney calcification brought on by the ingestion of so much vitamin D. When vitamin D fortification of baby foods was restricted, some cases of rickets again appeared.

Another example is found in the cholesterol controversy of more recent years. Although this "steroid" has an effect on the arteries, no general remedy has been found because some people are susceptible to fats, some to carbohydrates.

We seem to have genetic food needs as well as blood types, eye color, and so on. Perhaps these stem logically from whom we are descended from, where our ancestors lived, and what they ate.

The Right Amount of Food

As many overweight people have often felt, *over*nourishment in childhood is now thought by some nutritionists to result in an excessive number of fat cells, which ever after continue to cry out for nourishment, thus making their owners perpetually hungry—and perpetually fat if they lack the necessary will power to control their food intake. Between the starving and the indulging

Peace Corps Volunteer Jane Lovelady, 24, of Ransom, Kansas, works in San Mateo on the island of Luzon on a nutrition program in the barrio, using beans and greens grown by the farmers and prepared by the mothers for the children.
Peace Corps

there must be a happy food-intake medium. How much food is enough?

For computing world food needs, the United Nations Food and Agriculture Organization calculated the weight of a standard "reference man" as 65 kilograms, or about 143 pounds. Suggested caloric intake on this basis is 3,200 calories for the reference man. Averaged out for women at 55 kilograms, with children calculated proportionately, the global requisite is 2,354 calories per day per capita.

There are some who think the reference man is too well fed. In England the *Economist* has called FAO "a permanent institution devoted to proving that there is not enough food in the world." This comment came after an FAO study showed that 10 to 15 percent of the people in the world were hungry, and another 35 to 40 percent were undernourished. And Colin Clark faulted studies by FAO claiming that caloric intakes of ten- to fifteen-year-old Ceylonese boys proved they were underfed. Clark says that since the boys were of the middle and upper class they were probably not going hungry but eating about as much as they wanted or needed.

The President's Scientific Advisory Committee believes that perhaps people do need fewer calories than FAO estimates, but also fears they are not *getting* even that amount. Even more critical is the protein requirement, and it is estimated by SAC that at least one-fourth and perhaps as many as one-third of the people in undeveloped countries are protein deficient. FAO recommends about seventy grams of protein a day. SAC believes that the greatest protein deficiency occurs in preschool children, and in pregnant and nursing women, since these three groups should have more protein proportionately.

Although it has long been known that children require greater amounts of protein in proportion to body weight than adults because the young are still growing, one of the most important of recent nutrition findings is that malnutrition in infancy and early childhood can cause mental retardation. This has definitely been demonstrated in rats deprived of milk. Lack of milk prior to weaning causes a permanent restriction on the number of brain cells. After weaning, a restricted diet seems not to affect the number of brain cells. Proof is harder to come by in human young, since it is possible and probable that social deprivation—which usually accompanies malnutrition—may be as strong or even a stronger factor in mental retardation.

Simply by dividing known production of proteins by population we might be lulled into believing that everyone is getting enough. However, it is known that the developed countries eat from fifty-five to seventy-five grams of protein daily, while in undeveloped lands the intake ranges from five to fifteen grams.

Malnutrition

It is remarkable that a normal person maintains his weight with little conscious effort or care in meal planning. He just "naturally" eats the proper amount and the proper kinds of food. Some physiologists hypothesize a control called an "appestat" in the brain that dictates what and how much we eat. Tales of pregnant women who crave certain foods are indications of the body knowing what it needs for good nutrition. Yet tragically many people—the old, particularly—do not seem to have this natural feeling for a proper diet and subsist on easy-to-eat but not particularly healthful foods.

Too little nourishment or improper nourishment forces the body to feed on itself; ultimately such self-consumption could be fatal. As one wit has said, "Starvation is nature's way of telling us to eat more!" The nutrition chain has been diagramed as follows: Deficient nutrition → lowered energy output → lowered production → bare subsistence → meager education → decreased resistance to disease → high death rates among children → lowered life expectancy.

The United States has made great progress in nutrition from the year 1928 when some 7,000 Americans died of pellagra, a disease caused by deficiencies in protein and niacin. By 1946 this toll had been slashed to about 800, and in 1967 only 13 died of this disease. It is startling to realize, however, that even 13 died of a malnutritional disease. Actually, more than 2,100 people were recorded as dying from malnutrition and related causes in 1967 in the United States.

"Marasmus" is the medical term for what most of us consider starvation—death from a lack of food, gross starvation. There were no cases of marasmus reported in the United States in 1967, and many of the others were difficult to recognize as related to hunger. Senators at the Nutrition and Human Needs hearings in

U.S. Deaths Relating to Malnutrition (1967)

Malnutrition unqualified	1,274
Nutritional maladjustment	299
Hunger, thirst, exposure	193
Other and multiply defined states	143
Iron deficiency anemias	116
Dehydration	39
Steatorrhea and sprue	27
Lack of care, infants under 1	22
Pellagra	13
Kwashiorkor	11
Beriberi	8
Osteomalacia	4
Vitamin B deficiency	4
Scurvy	1
Rickets	1
Total	2,158

SOURCE: "Nutrition and Human Needs," U.S. Senate Hearings, August 1969.

September 1969 objected that most of the dead listed by one state exceeded seventy years of age and had probably died of other causes. Examples were a sixty-eight-year-old District Court marshal, whom Senator Allen Ellender objected surely had a good enough salary to sustain him. And when a ninety-three-year-old woman was reported as having died of cachexia, a malnutritional disease, Ellender cried "She died of old age!"

In some parts of the world marasmus is prevalent, however. It is not only loss of appetite that causes malnutrition or starvation, of course. With most who starve it is a matter of economics—of not having the money to buy food. Or if money is available it is not enough to buy sufficient protein. For example, a worker in Guatemala would have to spend 60 percent of his daily wage to buy one pound of beef! Those not quite as unlucky as marasmus sufferers get kwashiorkor.

Kwashiorkor is the other most prevalent disease, caused by lack of milk in the child's diet. Surprisingly, eleven victims were listed for the United States in 1967. *Kwashiorkor* is a Ghanian term,

Doris Bucher, left, of Myerstown, Pennsylvania, and Carol Neely, of
East Lansing, Michigan, prepare muffins to be eaten by a group of
student volunteers in a research experiment made to determine if
mealtime routines affect weight gains. The research was done at the
U.S. Department of Agriculture's Human Nutrition Laboratory with
fifteen coed volunteers.
USDA

meaning literally "displaced child," one taken from the breast
and having to fend for food. Well-known around the world, the
disease is called "sugar baby" in Jamaica, *enfant rouge* or "red
baby" in the Cameroons, *culebrilla* in Mexico, *polycarencil infantile* in Central America, *Mehlnahrschaden* in Germany—and
there are thirty-two other names for it elsewhere.

Hunger or malnutrition can also cause measles (which is a
hundred times as prevalent among children in India as in the
United States), goiter, anemia, beriberi, scurvy, rickets, and
pellagra, although these are not seen nearly as often as marasmus
or kwashiorkor.

The human body is a miraculous machine that has even accom-
modated itself to insufficient food. When we eat too much we get
fat. When we starve we get thin. The vicious hunger cycle goes
something like this: The less a person eats, the smaller he gets and
thus the less he needs to eat—so that he gets a little smaller yet.
Frederick Hulse comments in *The Human Species* on this evidence of adaptation in humans faced with not enough food:

A reduction in body size has often followed the development of intensive grain agriculture and may be a reflection of nutritional stress.
Newman (1960) has analyzed the relationship between average weight,
ambient temperature, and caloric intake among many tribes of American Indians. In the temperate and arctic areas, he found a regression
of average weight on the temperature of the coldest month. These
have been areas where the dependence on agriculture was far from
complete; in many cases no food crops at all were raised. The peoples
of Mexico, Central America, and Peru have cultivated maize for several thousand years, and it became their staple food long ago. Studies
by nutritionists show that the caloric intake has been very low indeed
for most people in this region. Protein and vitamin deficiencies exist.
The average weight falls well below what would be expected as a
response to climate alone. Growth and maturation are delayed among
these tribes and adult body size reduced. As an adaptation to the conditions of life, this makes good sense. Selection has probably removed
children who could not get along on what would be, for us, a most
inadequate diet.

In Uruguay, where the average food consumption is an estimated 3,030 calories daily, average height is 67 inches and weight
154 pounds. In Ecuador, where the calorie intake is only 2,100 per
day, height is 63 inches and weight 126 pounds. Between World
War I and World War II, American draftees gained almost 11
pounds in weight and 2.4 inches in height. And from 1948 to 1960
the Japanese people on the average gained 6 pounds and more
than 2 inches.

Just how size equates with health, and just what is the optimum
size for humans remains to be seen, of course. In fact, some tests
with mice indicated that those kept on a small intake of food were
healthier. They matured more slowly, which is understandable,

but lived longer—which shoots this approach down as a way to save food, since people who live longer consume more food in the long run.

As we become richer, we do not eat much more, measured in bulk or weight, than a subsistence cultivator living on grain—indeed, it would hardly be physically possible for us to do so. But we eat food from higher on the pyramid. Food consumed by the average North American or Western European amounts to ten or eleven "subsistence units," while the Japanese, with almost as good a health record, consume agricultural products at the rate of not much more than two "subsistence units" per head. This is because the Japanese must be content with a diet of rice, vegetables, and a small quantity of fish, not very different from that of their ancestors. As quickly as they can, however, the Japanese are "improving" their diet.

Great extremes exist in food and its supply. In some parts of the world, as we have seen, many are going hungry every day, with children dying of kwashiorkor. But in the United States, where the food business exceeds $75 billion a year, many households *waste* enough food to support another family, pay $1.50 a pound for potatoes (in the form of chips that are not particularly good for us because of the grease in them), and spend fortunes on so-called diet foods scientifically designed *not* to do what food is generally eaten to accomplish. The orgiastic Romans induced vomiting so that they could overindulge their palates. We, more fastidiously but perhaps as grossly, gorge ourselves on "low-cal" foods so as not to gain weight—while others starve for lack of food.

As a youngster I was constantly prodded to clean my plate, because "there are many less-fortunate people starving in the world." Just how my eating all my food was to help these poor people escaped me then, and the problem has still not been answered to this day. Good intentions are to be commended, but

COMPOSITION OF DIETS REFLECTS RISING NATIONAL INCOMES

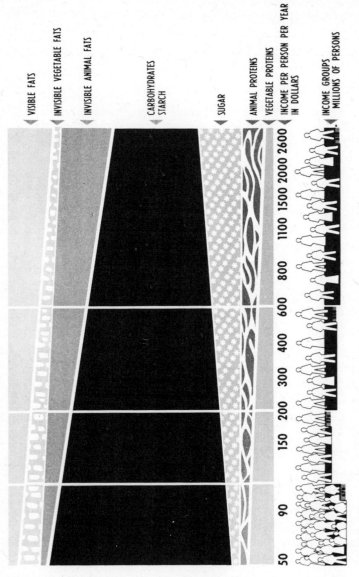

VISIBLE FATS

INVISIBLE VEGETABLE FATS

INVISIBLE ANIMAL FATS

CARBOHYDRATES STARCH

SUGAR

ANIMAL PROTEINS

VEGETABLE PROTEINS

INCOME PER PERSON PER YEAR IN DOLLARS

INCOME GROUPS MILLIONS OF PERSONS

50 90 150 200 300 400 600 800 1100 1500 2000 2600

Economics is a key factor in malnutrition. As this chart shows, consumers in the developing countries are short of protein, sugar, and fats. Wealthy nations eat too much of the latter two foods.
FAO

the problem of spreading out the plenty of food produced today so that all get a sufficient and nutritious amount is perhaps the knottiest problem facing us. Yet how difficult, in conscience, to do less than our best to alleviate hunger or even starvation in the world.

It is not known where he who invented the plough was
born or where he died, yet he has affected more the
happiness of the world than the whole race of heroes
and conquerors who have drenched it with tears and
manured it with blood.

John L. Blake

CHAPTER 7

Our Daily Bread

Today an acre of hybrid corn in the United States averages sixty
bushels and an acre of wheat in the Netherlands also averages
sixty bushels, perhaps as much more productive than yields in
Malthus's time as those yields in turn exceeded crop production
by the primitive tiller of the soil. Many things have boosted the
yield of plants man uses for food. Mechanization has worked
wonders, as has chemical treatment of soil, plants, and pests. Irrigation, and improved harvesting, handling, and storage have also
contributed. So well have all these approaches worked that the
McGraw-Hill Encyclopedia of Science and Technology gives
this appraisal of conditions in the United States:

In contrast to the situation in the so-called underdeveloped areas
of the world, where a large proportion of the world's population resides, agriculture in the United States has more than kept pace with
the growing need for its products. The situation is one of chronic
peacetime excess rather than of inadequate production, and most ob-
servers agree that the time for concern regarding ability to meet food
needs is not near at hand in the United States.

Our situation was not always this bright, nor is that of some of
the less fortunate this bright today.

Food Through the Ages

Broadly there have been three major food-securing periods. First was *hunting and gathering*. Man ate small animals, fowl, fish, berries, nuts, and fruit as he found them—raw. Next came *cooking*, perhaps stumbled onto by accident but leading to tastier food, available to more people. Finally, there is *food-producing*, in contrast to simply gathering what nature has provided.

Actually, the gathering of fruits, berries, nuts, and other such foods probably antedated hunting and killing for food. The first men were doubtless vegetarians. Any animals that were eaten were most likely insects or other small creatures of various kinds, bugs, snails, and so on. For one reason or another—some anthropologists suggest the shrinking of habitable forest areas—it became necessary or of benefit for early man to turn to hunting game for survival. Now he had added a rich, higher-protein food to his diet, although we would hardly be comfortable eating what our ancestors ate and in the manner they ate it. Food was most likely eaten on the spot it was picked up, and it was eaten raw. However, it might have been warm or even hot as it was bolted down.

Using rocks and sticks as weapons, and later as tools, man improved as a hunter and trapper. He may even have begun to keep game on the hoof, as a primitive storage method, until he had need of it. This was not yet domestication, but it was a step from the chase and gave him a more regular supply of meat. The extent to which the hunting urge permeated his culture and man himself is evident even today. This atavistic desire to take up gun or fishing rod and go forth to procure food is in most of us, and some food is taken in this way even by the most civilized.

Botanist Paul Mangelsdorf says that the first eating of grains was doubtless as popped corn or parched grain. This freed the cereals from their inedible husks and made them easier and tastier to eat. Next came grinding the parched kernels and making gruel

McCormick's wonderful reaper, which sparked a revolution of food production in 1857.
USDA

in water. This must have been a lifesaving invention for young, old, and toothless alike. Also, a gruel allowed to stand would become infected with wild yeasts and ferment. It is not known which came first, brewing or bread-making, but both have been used since their discovery. Early recipes for Egyptian beer describe a process that stems from bread-making, half-baked loaves being used as the raw material. In time this led to other kinds of cooking, including that of meat.

Different explanations have been advanced for the introduction of cooking. One theory is that it sought to duplicate "prey temperature" of the old meat-eating customs. Another claims that it made food tastier to eat and digest. Finally it is pointed out that cooking added flavor, appealing to the increasingly sophisticated palates of the cooks.

The third food phase, the one we are in, came when man for whatever reason began to cultivate plants for food. This "revolution" may have come about fortuitously; perhaps it paralleled the domestication of animals, or it could have been forced on man by growing population or natural changes in his habitual hunting or gathering grounds. Whatever the reason, agriculture worked powerful changes on everything from man's diet to his society. In short, it made possible the civilization we know.

At first agriculture amounted simply to the tending of the wild plants men found edible. Fruit and nut trees, berry bushes, and patches of vegetables and grains were cleared of weeds and protected from animal depredations. Slowly the ideas of transplanting and of planting seeds came into being, as did irrigation in areas of insufficient or irregular rainfall.

Egypt's Nile delta is a classic example of an irrigation culture, and millions of Egyptians have earned livelihoods as *fellahin*, or irrigators. In our American Southwest the Indians centuries ago dug crude but effective canals—some of which are still being used today—to channel river water across miles of dry desert to cultivated fields.

The first farming probably consisted of planting grains near the cave or hut, after a woman—women were the first farmers— had noticed that seeds spilled from pots they were being carried in sprang up along the trail. Holes and ditches were most likely dug with bare hands; irrigation water was carried in skins or pots from nearby streams.

Slowly the idea of tools came to the early farmers. A properly curved and pointed stick dug holes and trenches better. Water would flow down a man-made ditch much as it would in a river bed. The technique of plowing the soil was adopted, first using man—or woman—power, and later that of animals. Stones were lashed to sticks to make axes, shovels, hoes, and plows. The iron age provided stronger and more durable implements.

Farming led to the concept of property ownership—a new territoriality. Land meant a living, and formed a "real" base that could be taxed by lords or kings. Slowly farming changed from an occupation that everyone engaged in on subsistence plots, to a specialized business for farmers. With invention and mechanization, plus scientific understanding of agriculture, a farmer could produce enough for himself and have some left over for sale nearby, or even in distant places. Pumps and windmills appeared, along with sugar- and gristmills and cotton gins, as inventors got busy.

In England the "enclosures," relatively small, hedged fields, moved farming toward more efficiency. Industrialization and the growth of cities created new demands for food even as they took away many of the farmers. But those remaining in the fields could now supply two or three families or more.

In 1839 the United States Government gave the Patent Office the munificent sum of $1,000 for collecting and distributing seeds, and for research and statistical analysis of farming in this country. By 1862, in the throes of the Civil War, a Department of Agriculture had been set up, headed by a commissioner.

The use of slave labor on farms carried over to the plantations of America, until the Civil War wiped out slavery—and almost wiped out the single crop, cotton, the South was geared to. Mechanization soon began with a vengeance in America, and reapers, threshers, and combines cultivated the West with improved speed and efficiency. Man had earlier yielded his place before the plow to the horse, mule, or ox; now animals began to be turned out to pasture. In a mechanized world, snorting, smoking tractors carried the internal combustion engine into the fields as automobiles put them on the roads and highways.

Farming in primitive times must have been somewhat like trying to live on piñon nuts—in both cases one would have to work at it continuously to keep from starving to death. Science and technology slowly eased that pressure, and by the time the United States saw fit to include the Agriculture Department head in the President's cabinet in 1889, one American farmer could supply the needs of five other people. Today one American farmer can feed more than forty.

Not all of this productivity can be attributed to excellent

management. In the 1930s, for example, poor farming techniques teamed with drought and wind to create a bleak Dust Bowl in our Midwest. We are still saddled with subsidies, soil banks, and other difficult-to-explain methods of payment for land plowed under and little pigs butchered to keep them from going to market. And before we boast too much of farming efficiency in our country, we should recall that a good "European diet" in Europe requires about one acre of land per person, only half an acre in Japan—and one and a half acres in the United States. Our agriculture is by no means the most efficient or productive in the world.

Malthus would be amazed, and doubtless relieved, to see the improvement in food production since his time. It is science and technology that deserve most of the credit for increased yields and better-quality crops. Several distinct factors have contributed to the improvement of agriculture in the last century, including mechanization, irrigation, fertilization, pest and weed control, and plant genetics.

The Mechanization of Farming

It is possible to plow a field with man or mule power, to plant by hand, and to harvest in the same manner. It is not very profitable, however, and without mechanization one man cannot feed many others, as farmers in developed countries are now able to do. In many parts of the world such mechanization is not available, for various reasons. It might seem questionable how much better a job a tractor can do than a water buffalo in a rice paddy, for example. But contrast the planting, watering, and harvesting of wheat as it was done in Biblical times—and as it is still done in some lands today—with the highly mechanized techniques used on modern farms.

In 1800 the grain "cradle" began to be used generally in the United States and some other farming areas. A worker using a cradle, with another man to help him by raking and binding the

Irrigation can spell the difference between life and death for the farmers of Upper Volta. Irrigation techniques are therefore high on the list of new methods taught at the agricultural center by FAO experts.
FAO photo by A. Defever

grain, could cut from two to two and a half acres a day. Then came the grain reaper, and by 1852 a competitive test showed that nine men using a reaper could match the output of fourteen cradlers. The reaper in turn gave way to the combine, introduced in about 1880. By the 1930s a combine could harvest twenty-five acres a day, and thresh the grain while it was about it. This represented a gain of almost seventy-five times in efficiency over the earlier cradle and flail method. Now one man with a combine can harvest enough wheat in a day to make one-third of a million loaves of bread.

Cotton was a handpicking crop until the mechanized picker came along. As anyone who has tried it knows, handpicking ten or fifteen pounds of cotton in an hour is back-breaking work.

But the cottonpicker on wheels, with a motor driving its grasping fingers, picks a 500-pound bale in little over an hour. Today there are also machines that glean what the picker misses, even salvaging it from the ground. Peanuts can be produced in shelled condition at the rate of about one pound an hour by human hands. A mechanized harvester cranks out 300 pounds of shelled peanuts in the same amount of time. A Chinese farmer can plant a one-acre rice paddy in something like a week—if he works fourteen hours a day all seven days. California rice growers plant fifty acres in an hour—from an airplane! A good celery-plant setter puts out about 7,500 plants in a day. Two men with a transplanting machine can do 40,000 of the plants in the same length of time.

Mechanization allows a farmer to work fast in good weather, so that bad weather is less a problem than it once was. Electrification of farms has given better means of pumping, drying, processing, and storage. Loading and unloading operations are mechanized, with hoisting done by electric winch instead of man or animal power.

Irrigation

In the old days farmers tilled the soil of river deltas to be near water, or relied on rainfall despite the danger of drought and flood. Water was pumped by animal or manpower, or at best by windmill. Canals were hand dug, and subject to silting and clogging with vegetation. The Babylonian civilization waned, for example, choked in dust and silt when its water systems failed.

Mechanization also provided better well-drilling equipment, and this helped agriculture. Ancient farmers dug some majestic wells by hand, but today a well-drilling rig can punch a hole neatly and rapidly to great depths, bringing up water from hundreds of feet below the surface. In fact, California and Texas fruit, cotton, and winter vegetable crops can be profitably irrigated from depths of 500 hundred feet and more. In general crop production,

100 feet is about maximum, unless specialized irrigation techniques such as sprinkling are used.

About one-third of the crops in the United States come from irrigated farms, and irrigated land yields from two to three times as much produce per acre as does unirrigated land. In California, 85 percent of the crops are irrigated. Even in Oregon and Washington, thought of as rainy states, 35 percent and 45 percent, respectively, of the crops are irrigated. In Utah and Wyoming, from 75 to 85 percent of the farming is done under irrigation; in Nevada and Arizona, where rain is a novelty, nearly all farming is irrigated; and of the eight mountain states, 60 percent of the farming is on irrigated land.

When considering food-population problems and solutions it is well to remember that water is limited, too, and that a water shortage may limit food production. In many areas water tables are dropping because of overdrafts made for irrigation of fields. Such "mining" of water cannot continue indefinitely. In other areas the water is too contaminated with harmful minerals to be useful even for irrigation. Piping in water over long distances, or desalinating brackish supplies or seawater will add greatly to the cost of agriculture.

Fertilization

It is doubtful that primitive farmers knew that plants cannot fix nitrogen from the air or soil except through the help of bacteria at their roots, or that they realized that nitrogen was desirable to increase crop yields. Men farmed for thousands of years before nitrogen was discovered. However, it was inevitable as they plowed their fields that manure be accidentally added to the soil from place to place. When some bright farmer saw the connection between an especially productive plant and cattle or horse droppings in the area, the principle of fertilizing plants was born. For thousands of years manure—animal and human— has been applied to the soil. Containing water, carbon dioxide, and most importantly nitrogen, phosphorus, and potassium, manure aids in plant growth. The poet Virgil wrote in his "Art of Husbandry" in 30 B.C.:

> Yet sprinkle sordid ashes all around
> And load with fattening dung thy fallow ground.

Here man was only doing selectively what nature's ecological system had been doing for ages—returning nitrogen to green plants so they could produce the carbohydrates and oxygen needed by man. Just as rotting vegetation acts to fertilize soil for future growth, so decomposing animal matter does the same.

By the time Columbus reached North America, the Indians had long been using fish as fertilizer. Fish residue yields up to 10 percent nitrogen, 8 percent phosphorus, and 1 percent potassium, and thus is an excellent fertilizer, although just how ancient farmers stumbled onto this fact is not quite sure. Nor did the Indians and others who tossed fish into the ground when they planted grains of corn know that they were being most wasteful in this juggling of the food chain. Since fish represents the top of the marine food pyramid of several levels, and the refinement of the original source of green plant life of plankton into a fraction of 1 percent of its original caloric value, the Indians would seem to have done better to eat the fish. However, with a surplus of fish and a shortage of corn, the ecologically wasteful practice was justified.

It was several centuries after Columbus that the German chemist and pioneer in agricultural science, Justus von Liebig, established the validity of artificially supplementing the nutrients in soil with chemicals—namely, lime, phosphate, and potash. This was about the time of the introduction of firearms, and to provide explosives, since gunpowder also depended on nitrates, pigeon lofts were raided and other bird and animal droppings were sought out and in time Chile became a big supplier of both gunpowder and fertilizer, two rather diverse uses for a product. The developing chemical industry also provided sources of fertilizers, and the coking of coal produced by-products like ammonium sulfate. Eventually the brilliant German chemist Fritz Haber developed a method of "fixing" nitrogen from the atmosphere, thus assuring Germany a steady supply of nitrate explosives for World War I and farmers ample fertilizer ever afterward.

One hundred bushels of corn taken from a field also removes about 78 pounds of nitrogen, 36 pounds of phosphoric oxide, and 26 pounds of potassium oxide. Additional amounts of 52, 18, and 94 pounds, respectively, are removed in the fodder. Thus 100 bushels of corn takes more than 300 pounds of fertilizer from the soil.

For a long time fertilization was thought to be merely the matter of replenishing those constituents taken up from the soil by growing plants. But plant science learned that this method of simply dumping in the quantities thought needed for replacement was only a crude application of the principle of fertilization. It was found, for example, that certain chemical elements stimulated plant growth beyond normal. Nitrogen in particular had the ability to produce more vegetable growth, or to make a plant put more of its energies into reproductive activities. Thus, not only could fertilizers induce growth, they could control and vary it.

Slowly the agricultural chemists learned that in addition to the known nutrients nitrogen, phosphorus, and potassium, there were "secondary" nutrients, including calcium, magnesium, and sulfur. Chlorine and iron were also found to be useful, but in much smaller amounts.

At the turn of the last century a breakthrough was made in agricultural chemistry. Japan, with its great overcrowding, was diligent in this field, and in 1901 a researcher named M. Nagaoka applied various minerals to plants and found that manganese was a marked stimulant for rice, a most important crop in Japan. Some ten years later, German agricultural scientist E. Hazelhoff used boron with similar results on a number of other plants. Since that time, further testing has demonstrated that copper, molybdenum,

Local way of fertilizing pastures. Modern machinery, however, is being rapidly introduced into Ecuador where this picture was made.
FAO

and zinc are also essential mineral elements. Thus, in addition to the primary and secondary nutrients, now called "macronutrients," seven "micronutrients" are also known and used. Despite the small quantities of the latter, they are very important.

Just as men and animals suffer from shortages of needed minerals, so do plants. A damaging condition in cauliflower called "whiptail" comes from a molybdenum deficiency. Many deciduous fruits suffer leaf-dwarfing and other deficiencies when insufficient zinc is available to them. Zinc deficiency also attacks to cause dwarfing and "sickle leaf" in cacao, and it stunts the growth of beans. "Mouse ear," or wrinkling of pecan leaves, can be cured by adding manganese to orchard soil. Too little copper causes few or no seeds in tomatoes. Boron in too small quantities causes "brown heart" on the roots of beets, rutabagas, and turnips;

"blossom blast" on pears; poor setting of cotton bolls; and gum deposits in citrus.

Since the discovery of the need for the trace minerals, it has been found that half the soil in the United States is naturally deficient in manganese, and almost a third is deficient in copper. Fortunately, a light application of the minerals generally suffices, and as little as a pound per acre may last up to thirty years. Here was a tremendous and cheaply applied boon to agricultural production.

Chemical application can be a mixed blessing, however. For example, it is a practice to apply lime to overly acid soils to neutralize them, but the overliming of soils in Florida caused a dangerous side effect: plants increased the amounts of molybdenum they absorbed to the point that they became toxic to animals feeding on them!

In the United States, the use of fertilizers in agriculture long ago passed the $1 billion a year mark, and by 1975 the amount is expected to double. In return, about 25 percent of the crop yield is attributed to these artificial fertilizers.

The Growth Regulators

We have seen that fertilizer applied to the soil works into the roots of plants and can affect growth and development. Sprays from the air can do the same thing, and "growth regulation" has become part of agricultural chemistry. Long before men knew about chemical science, they learned by accident and observation that certain things enhanced the growth of fruit and other plants. For example, tenders of fig orchards in the Near East somehow found out that a drop of olive oil in the eye of a fully developed but still green fig would cause it to ripen as much as two weeks earlier than nature could do the job. The Japanese learned by similar serendipitous discovery that storing persimmons briefly in an old sake cask removed the "puckering" quality of the fruit and made them sweeter.

For centuries nobody knew why such tricks worked, or worried much about it. They worked, that was all, and farmers made use of the fact. But around the turn of the century curious agricultural scientists began experimenting on artificial ripening of this sort. When it was found that the sake cask reeked with ethylene gas, tomatoes in the United States were exposed to ethylene obtained from sources other than sake casks, and they ripened more quickly. The trick also worked on some other fuits and vegetables, but not all.

If science could speed ripening, could it also slow it down? Some things, like potatoes and onions, sprouted too rapidly while in storage. So various chemicals were sprayed on them, and it was found that the vapor of isopropyl carbamate inhibited sprouting in potatoes in storage and maleic hydrazide sprayed on growing potatoes and onions a few weeks before harvesting also delayed sprouting.

Other growth regulators prevent fruit from dropping prematurely from trees, and inhibit strawberry runners and tobacco plant suckers. The Japanese have demonstrated that "gibberellins" cause greatly increased vegetative growth, and that fumaric acid dwarfs plants. Other treatment can artificially pollinate figs and seedless grapes. Gibberellins, incidentally, were first discovered by Japanese scientists investigating diseased rice.

The Pesticides We Can't Do Without

In all the condemnation of pesticides—some of it merited, of course—there is a tendency to overlook or to forget the great part that pesticides have played in increasing production and improving the quality of the crop. In the earliest literature great plagues of locusts, grasshoppers, and other insects are described. Many Irish are in this country because of the great potato famines in Ireland in 1846 and 1847, when a fungus blighted the staple food of that country. In America grasshoppers, worms, and other pests have ruined crops periodically, and in undeveloped countries crop losses to pests and weeds may well run to 40 percent and more.

Even now in the United States a sizable portion of crops are lost between planting and use. Accurate statistics are difficult to arrive at, and the accompanying table published by the Scientific Advisory Committee may be double the actual losses. However, even half this much is a heavy price to pay to pests and weeds—something like 25 million *tons* of food.

Percent of Crop Lost in United States 1951–60

	INSECTS	DISEASE	WEEDS	TOTAL LOSS
Maize	12	12	10	34
Wheat	6	14	12	32
Rice	4	7	17	28
Grain sorghum	9	9	13	31
Soybean	8	14	17	39
Potato	14	19	3	36

The information that man has upset the ecological balance and that pests increased as the available supply of their favored food was increased and concentrated into efficient farms is no news and little comfort to the farmer. Because of this upset he has for centuries had to rid himself of the various pests that invade and devour his living. Quoting Virgil again:

> Yet even upon the grain fell plague, erelong
> Mildew defiled the stalks, and everywhere
> The barbed thistles gathered in lawless throng
> Till villainous weeds displaced the harvest there.

Pest poisons initially consisted of spells and incantations, evolving into witches' brews and similar nostrums more psychological than scientific. But there were early poisons, too. It is quite probable that primitive men noted the killing effects of salt water and applied this as a simple weed killer. The efficacy of sulfur was also noted in early writing on agricultural pests. But the era of scientific pesticides was relatively late in coming.

1968 locust invasion in Ethiopia. More than 40 countries, from West Africa to North India, were threatened by the worst outbreak of locust plague since 1959.
FAO, Rome

Among the first was Paris green, used in 1860 by desperate Colorado farmers when the potato beetle threatened to repeat the Irish catastrophe in America. The poison was so effective that other arsenic-containing chemicals were tried, with increasing success. Indeed, by 1890 lead arsenate was a standard pesticide. Other popular poisons used were the oil emulsions effective against sucking insects.

During World War II a new tool appeared in the form of DDT, merciful acronym for a long-known and complex chemical compound. First used by the military for killing disease-carrying insects, DDT was soon taken over enthusiastically by farmers, dairymen, and home-owners as an insect killer par excellence. DDT unfortunately turned out to be a mixed blessing: insects evolved protective mechanisms against the stuff, and DDT proved so lastingly persistent as to be considered by some a danger to living things, including man. It is now beginning to be banned.

However, DDT had a remarkable success in killing insects. When it was adopted in the Pacific Northwest, farmers, who had had to spray about 2,000 gallons of pesticides per acre to kill invaders, found that only 600 gallons of DDT per acre were needed. The new chemical also cut costs about 50 percent. Since DDT, newer pesticides such as chlordane, dieldrin, aldrin, and the very effective and dangerous parathion have been developed and are in heavy use.

These chemicals kill insects, but not fungus. Another chemical approach was necessary to fight these microscopic food-devourers. About the time that farmers in the United States were developing their oil sprays for bugs, French grape growers accidentally discovered the effective "Bordeaux mixture." Seeking a preparation to spray on grapes to make them look poisoned and discourage theft, the growers put together lime and copper sulfate. Not only did the stuff scare off grape-nappers, it also killed the fungi that damaged the vineyards. The Bordeaux mixture was adapted to other fruits, and has been improved to eliminate many harmful side effects that developed.

Nematodes, tiny roundworms that infest the roots of plants, not only do great damage to crops but were found to carry virus diseases, thus providing a double reason for eliminating them. Nematocides, principally composed of ethylene dibromide, have provided much more effective control of nematodes than the earlier attempts at steaming the soil.

The irradiation technique that preserves produce after harvesting has also been used to sterilize animal pests, the best-known example being the screwworm fly. By irradiating the males with sources of nuclear energy and then releasing them by the millions to mate with normal females, the fly has been all but wiped out. Thus much of the livestock that would previously have been diseased or killed by the young of the screwworm fly, hatched in cuts on the animals, have been saved. The bollworm that destroys

A jar containing moths used in research is examined by Dr. Edward F. Knipling, director of the Entomology Research Division of the Department of Agriculture's Research Division, and pioneer in sterilization techniques to eliminate insect pests.
USDA photo by Murray Lemmon

cotton is now being treated in this way, as are other pests. Here is a method safer than the spraying of chemical pesticides that can, and sometimes do, destroy benign life types and even damage property and poison food.

Herbicides

As every gardener and lawn-tender knows, weeds sometimes do better than the crops or grass. Historically man has battled these unwanted invaders of field and yard with his bare hands, a hoe, or even fire, or buried them with mulch. Herbicides, or chemical

weed killers—principally sodium arsenite, another arsenic poison—
were known in the nineteenth century, and later such chemicals as
TCA (sodium trichloroacetate) were developed for completely
killing all the vegetation in courtyards, driveways, railroad rights-
of-way, and so on. About the time DDT came into use, so did
the potent new weed killer 2,4-D (short for 2,4-dichlorophenoxy-
acetic acid). TCA killed plants by burning up tissues, while 2,4-D
produced abnormal development, much like a cancerous growth,
that caused the plant to die.

A few thousand acres were treated with herbicides in 1940;
today tens of millions of acres are so treated. Often applied by
aircraft, 2,4-D and other chemicals control weeds on railroad
tracks, highway rights-of-way, and, of course, farm fields. At
times proper precautions are not taken, and the spray drifts from
its intended target and harms adjacent crops, bees, and possibly
other living things. Not herbicides but also used as a chemical
tool in farming are the defoliants, which strip the foliage from
plants to facilitate picking operations.

Genetics

In 1857 an Austrian monk named Gregor Mendel painstakingly
began to perform thousands of experiments with pea plants, recording what happened as to color, shape, size, and so on, when
he crossbred this with that. Unsung during his own lifetime, Mendel nevertheless introduced the science of genetics, and botanists
and other scientists after him have continued to experiment with the
creation of hybrid types of plants—much as man had empirically
bred animals for a long time.

The results, including the boysenberries of Luther Burbank
and the much more important hybrids of corn and wheat, have
been impressive and economically important for agriculture.
Conservative estimates of the value of such juggling of plant
genes and chromosomes by crossbreeding indicate 750,000,000
bushels of corn and 250,000,000 bushels of wheat a year in added

yield. In corn this gain was accomplished by more productive strains; the wheat hybrids were varieties more resistant to disease and insect infestations.

Mark Alfred Carleton was an employee of the fledgling U.S. Department of Agriculture. From Russia he brought back two strains of wheat that proved hardy and productive in America, the Kubanka and the Kharkov. Ironically, Carleton died of malaria in a low-paying job in Peru at the age of fifty-nine, unhailed as an agricultural hero.

In Canada, Angus MacKay and others created the Marquis strain of wheat by crossbreeding Red Fife with other types. Closer to our time, and in the field of corn, George Harrison Shull and a better-known personage, Henry Wallace, produced amazing strains of corn that have boosted the output from American farms mightily.

The only major contribution to the science of agriculture in this century was the theory of "heterosis" developed by Shull, and its practical utilization by D. F. Jones in 1916. Heterosis is the hybrid vigor, or increase in size, yield, and performance found in hybrids.

Apparently, inbreeding gradually weakens a plant or, for that matter, an animal. By crossing two varieties, a stronger plant or animal is produced. The mule is cited as an example of hybrid vigor at the animal level. Unfortunately, mules are sterile. Plants, however, can be hybrid and produce seed for further plantings. What Jones did was to originate a highly beneficial "double cross," starting with four inbred strains to make two hybrids, then further crossing the hybrids. Today there are thousands of hybrid strains, and we shall see some of the results in a later chapter.

Plants for Food

In his long history as an eater, man has surely sampled thousands of kinds of plants. Many of these have undoubtedly produced regrettable results, but some 3,000 have sustained him—

everything from piñon nuts to pigweed, and dandelions to sun-
flower seeds, tickle the palate or simply fill an empty stomach.
However, from all the thousands of possibilities among the green
plants that convert sunshine and gas and water into solid organic
carbohydrates man has over the years settled on a baker's dozen
for most of his needs. These are wheat, rice, corn, sugar beets,
sugarcane, sweet potatoes, white potatoes, common beans, soybeans, cassavas, peanuts (which are actually roots, not nuts),
coconuts, and bananas.

Most of us have eaten all these at one time or another—cassava,
in case you'd forgotten, produces tapioca pudding—but some
cultures base their diet on a few, or perhaps even just one, of
these plants. Rice is the staple food of much of Asia, for example,
and sweet potatoes are regular fare for some South Americans
and South Sea Islanders.

Basic plant foods include: cereals (corn, wheat, barley, rye,
oats, rice, etc.); sugar (beets and cane); vegetables (potatoes,
sweet potatoes, cassava, beans, peas, onions, etc.); fruits (bananas,
berries, plantains, etc.); nuts (almonds, coconuts, etc.); bacteria
(molds, mushrooms, yeasts).

King Nebuchadnezzar found eating grass something better
suited to the animals. Grass, to most of us, is something to keep
off of in the park, to mow and weed, and that dries up if we fail
to water it enough in the hot summer months. But grass is man's
basic food, too, for the cereal grains are all "grasses."

Charred grains of wheat and barley, dating back almost 10,000
years, have been found in Iraq. The first civilizations we know of
in the Chaldees and Babylon depended mainly on wheat from the
"fertile crescent" between the Tigris and the Euphrates. The later
Egyptians, Greeks, and Romans added barley. China fed itself—
and still does—on rice. In the Western Hemisphere the Aztecs,
Incas, and Mayas among others cultivated corn, along with beans,
peppers, and squash.

Cereal grains are the standby crops, and provide about three-
quarters of the calorie needs of Asia, Africa, and Central and

Cassava, yams, taro, and groundnuts in a Bangkok market.
FAO photo by F. Botts

Latin America. Rice is the largest single contributor, furnishing 60 percent of the calories for half the world. It requires much water for cultivation, and cannot flourish in dry areas. In semiarid regions such as North China, Manchuria, and parts of India and Africa, sorghum and millet are the staple crops. From them come bread and mush, feeding a third of the world.

In the United States we grow some sorghum and millet, mostly as food for cattle. Wheat and corn thrive here and in many other lands with moderate rain and a temperate climate. Canada, the western portion of Europe, Russia, and parts of the Middle East grow much wheat and corn. Corn produces 3.2 million calories per acre, the highest of the cereals. However, since wheat yields better flour, more acreage is given over to it than to corn, whose meal is not as good for bread. Rye is grown in cold climates and poor soil, such as are found in northern Asia and Europe. So black loaves of rye bread are a staple in the diet of northern

Europe and the Scandinavian countries, and in the north portions of Russia.

Wheat is used almost entirely for flour to bake bread and other goods. Corn is more versatile. Sometimes known as "maize," it provides cornbread, hominy, grits, cornstarch, syrup, grain alcohol, sugar, and acetone. Corn is most used as an animal feed, however. Rye makes bread, liquor, and animal feed. Barley is used in brewing beverages, as a flavoring, and in breakfast foods. Oats feed animals and are also popular with humans as breakfast food. In his dictionary Dr. Samuel Johnson defined oats this way: "A grain which in England is generally given to horses, but in Scotland supports the people." Boswell, a Scot, did not take this jibe too well and later wrote triumphantly: "It was pleasant to me to find that 'Oats,' the 'food of horses,' were so much used as the food of the people in Dr. Johnson's own town."

In South America, and to some extent in Southeast Asia and other areas of the world, cereals give way to tubers or roots—the sweet potato, white potato, and cassava. These provide a starchy diet with plenty of sugar. While these tuberous plants are bulky to handle, high in water content, and easily spoiled, they are also easy to grow with primitive equipment and, in the case of sweet potatoes, also yield almost as high a caloric value per acre as corn. Sugarcane and beets are used to produce sugar, syrup, and molasses. An especially fine syrup also comes from the maple tree.

There are many vegetables other than the few staple kinds mentioned, of course. Cabbage, turnips, cucumbers, onions, olives, and tea plants were grown more than 4,000 years ago. Dating back to the time of Christ are carrots, celery, asparagus, lettuce, peas, and mustard seed.

Beans are an important vegetable since they contain large amounts of protein. Soybeans are particularly valuable in this regard: the beans are eaten as a vegetable, and soybean flour is used for making bread, thickening gravies, and many other things. More exotic garbanzo beans tickle sophisticated palates in some parts of the world, and in some places peanuts, also called "ground nuts," are prized when boiled in salted water, in which condition they are most reminiscent of beans.

Fruits are high in water content but are also a source of sugar, acids, and minerals. Apples are popular in much of the world, and are eaten raw, or are made into pies, jellies, cider, or are used in vinegar. Oranges and other citrus fruits are valuable for sugar and acids. The English long ago discovered the importance of citrus as a preventer of scurvy on shipboard, giving rise to the nickname of "lime-juicers," or simply "limeys," for British sailors.

Bananas, which are merely a popular fruit in this country, are staple items of diet in many lands. Berries, too, are popular fruits, both in their natural forms and as the hybrid types, like boysen-berries, created by plant geneticists.

Nuts, such as almonds, coconuts, pecans, walnuts, and the various seeds as well, are valuable sources of protein and also of fats, plus a fair amount of carbohydrates.

The Business of Farming

One secret of food plenty, fostered by competition and the profit motive, is an efficient food processing, storage, and delivery system. Traditionally the stockyards use every part of the pig but the squeal, and this approach applies to plant products as well. Rapid harvesting and modern packaging techniques use most of what is grown, with little waste in the fields or elsewhere.

Because of high-speed communication and transportation, plus sophisticated planning techniques that include computer analysis and control, quickly grown crops can be speedily shipped to meet demand that may vary from week to week and place to place. Surpluses are stored where possible, and minimum waste is incurred in the process.

Farming depends on the weather, and for centuries farmers' almanacs have attempted to prognosticate favorable planting and harvesting times. While there is some truth and scientific basis for doing things at certain times of the moon, modern farm science

Wheat combines harvesting in Nebraska. These represent a century of technological advance over the pioneering McCormick machines. *USDA*

depends more on meteorology than on old wives' tales and the occult.

The Department of Agriculture works with the Weather Bureau—now the Environmental Sciences Service Administration (ESSA)—and also with the World Meteorological Organization, on agricultural problems. With accurate measurement of temperature, humidity, and wind, and by closely monitoring crop conditions, farmers can more efficiently use irrigation water, pesticides, and herbicides and better plan their planting and harvesting times.

Many farmers today are graduates of agricultural schools, and many universities and land-grant colleges maintain large and active research facilities devoted to improvement of crops and methods. Farming is a science in the truest sense of the word, involving not only genetics and meteorology but chemistry, physics, and computer analysis, to name a few disciplines.

Food Processing

Moldy flour touched off the first LSD trip in history when European villagers were driven mad by eating bread baked from ergot-infected rye. Fortunately such harmful outbreaks are scarce, but at the very least moldy or otherwise infected food is of little use to hungry people. As pesticide treatment in the field is necessary to cut losses to bacteria, insects, and other pests, so similar chemical treatment or more sophisticated methods are needed to prevent loss during storage.

The techniques of food handling, manufacturing, processing, and distributing are generally lumped under the heading of "food engineering," a discipline that involves such sciences as chemistry, bacteriology, microbiology, mathematics, engineering, mechanics, and physics—and, not surprisingly, universities are turning out degreed "food engineers." Without food engineering, it has been pointed out that food would be available only on farms, in the forms produced by nature, and only in season.

Food preservation has progressed to a high state of perfection. Freezing, drying, freeze-drying, preserving, irradiation, and other processes are used to prevent spoilage and rotting. Microorganisms are what spoil food, and such organisms are destroyed by heating, freezing, or the newer practice of radiation. Although the processes have not been perfected, and some products such as fish and poultry do not yet lend themselves to sterilization by cobalt radiation or other such methods, many foods are thus rendered free of bacteria so they may be stored for long periods of time with no danger. Proponents of radiation sterilizing methods foresee the day when refrigeration will no longer be needed except for such things as ice cream, cold drinks, and so on. Even meats may be kept without freezing or canning for a year and more.

Continuous pressure cookers cook and sterilize processed foods on an automated basis.
USDA

In the old days man smoked meat or fish, or dried it. (Dehydration is still commonly used to preserve foods, as well as to reduce bulk, saving space and transportation costs.) Sometimes salt was added. But today there is a long list of chemical additives, all of them tested and regulated by the Food and Drug Administration, that aim at preserving, as well as at flavoring, coloring, adding nutritional value, and so on. There are acidulants, aerating agents, anticaking agents, antioxidants, bleaching agents, buffering agents, clarifying agents, clouding agents, color stabilizers, conditioners, emulsifiers, enzymes, flavors, foam regulators, humectants, hydrolytic agents, maturing agents, neutralizers, nutrients, preservatives, sweeteners, texturing agents, and thickeners.

Preservation is only one part of overall food engineering. Food processing changes a giant tuna fish into a can of choice white tuna meat available in the local supermarket, or turns the lowly potato into a more or less tasty chip that has been sliced, corrugated, seasoned, cooked, and bagged in an attractive package. Bread is a far cry from a sheaf of wheat, a form of food most of us would starve alongside of. Much processing is required to make such products as candy, ice cream, cheese, hot dogs, and cereals available and relatively unperishable in stores.

Food engineering includes the manufacturing of food products, some resembling natural foods, and some completely different from anything found in nature. Examples of manufactured foods are animal feeds, pet food, vegetable products in wide variety, fruit products, confections, bakery goods, sauces, meat products, poultry products, desserts, condiments and seasonings, sugar, flour of various kinds, frozen and powdered eggs and milk, chewing gum, fermented foods, soft drinks, and other drinks, including milk substitutes and artificial fruit drinks. And while some of us speak fondly of living close to nature and using natural foods prepared as nature intended them to be, most of us have been ably helped out of the kitchen by food engineers and the refined foods they have prepared. In the United States, as well as some other countries, a number of food products are fortified with minerals and vitamins to prevent deficiency diseases. Flour, bread, cornmeal and grits, farina, rice, pastina and macaroni products, for example, contain added amounts of thiamine, riboflavin, niacin, iron, calcium, and vitamin D.

Finally, packaging does much to facilitate transportation, storage, and selection, and to promote sales appeal. Glass and metal are being joined by paper, plastics, and other new packaging materials. There even seems to be some progress toward packaging that is more easily recycled or disposed of.

Problems in Underdeveloped Lands

Most of us in the United States are thoroughly indoctrinated in the modern food processing and distributing methods just discussed. In many developing portions of the world, on the other hand, modern food processing and distribution can be found only in isolated spots. Most areas rely on ancient methods subject to spoilage, loss to rats and other pests, and little or no variety of diet, including shortages of needed proteins, vitamins, and minerals.

It is unfortunate that the underdeveloped countries cannot produce food as efficiently and in the yields enjoyed in developed lands. This is, of course, one of the key reasons why such countries are underdeveloped. Mechanization, irrigation, fertilization, pesticides, and knowledge of plant breeding are in too short supply where they are most needed. This is the problem facing those who are trying to feed the world.

The reasons for shortcomings in agriculture are many. A poor economy is an obvious reason. A country with only a hundred dollars or so of per capita income can ill afford to spend millions or billions of dollars on irrigation projects, farm machinery, or farm chemicals, much as it might need those things to raise its income. Here is the paradox facing the have-nots: Them that have, get; them that don't have find it terribly hard to do so.

Three things that hamper agriculture in developing countries are tradition, culture, and superstition—all making it difficult to adopt or adapt to new methods of farming. And in lands where there is little education, agriculture can hardly be a science. Instead it remains more an art, and artists are generally hungry. The Scientific Advisory Committee lists five key reasons for the backwardness of agriculture in underdeveloped lands:

1. Lack of personnel properly trained for crop-production efforts.

2. Failure to emphasize yield per area and unit of time rather than per traditional crop-growing season.

3. Lack of ability on the part of developed nations in tropical agriculture.

4. The erroneous belief that agricultural technology can be transferred to tropical areas as effectively as principles of crop production.

Inflatable plastic warehouse built in Kenya for storing corn. Moisture-proof, it can also be fumigated to kill insects and other pests.
USDA

5. The reliance on donations of food, which has stifled local effort and discouraged what initiative farmers had.

The answer to these problems is patience and continuing education. It is unrealistic to expect production of crops in underdeveloped lands to rise quickly to biological limits rather than those imposed by economic and cultural considerations. But production must begin to bridge the existing gap if the growing numbers are to be fed.

"Who shall give us flesh to eat?"
Numbers 11:4

Meat—Can We Afford It?

There are about 1 billion cattle, 1 billion sheep, more than half a billion pigs, a third of a billion goats, 100 million water buffalo, and more than 130 million horses, mules, asses, and camels on Earth. In fact, there are almost as many meat animals in the world as there are humans. There are similar numbers of poultry, so man is far outnumbered by the animals he raises for food.

George Borgstrom goes much farther, by converting animals into "human equivalents" on the basis of their size and food consumption. He estimates that the animal population of the United States is equivalent to more than 1.3 billion humans. Thus we have a combined equivalent population of nearly 1.5 billion in this country right now, close to half the total human population of the entire world. Extending his figures worldwide, Borgstrom arrives at the sobering total of 15 billion human equivalents in the animal population. Put at its simplest, this means that if there were no animals there would be plant food enough to feed 15 billion more humans, enough for many decades into the future.

Borgstrom's estimates do not allow for animals other than livestock and draft animals. Pets, wildlife, rats, rabbits, snakes, and so on are an additional biomass and add more billions to the world population of animals. Although some shops carry lion meat and canned snake delicacies, most wild animals contribute nothing to the diet of human beings—and many tame ones are in the same category. Indeed, pets consume many tons of food in our country alone, and make an appreciable dent in the available worldwide supply. Cats, according to Borgstrom, consume about one-third of the canned fish in this country!

Borgstrom and others raise the question of feeding pets while much of the world goes hungry. As Borgstrom points out, there are no pets in China, a probable indication that pets exist in reverse proportion to a country's nutritional level. Dr. Harold E. Myers, Dean of the Agricultural College at the University of Arizona, dared to tackle this touchy question at the Annual International Turfgrass Conference in San Francisco in 1968:

One very real and direct way to save food for humans is to curtail our population of pets. A large, needy nation in Asia or Africa could be fed by the well-balanced array of calories which go into the cans and sacks of dog food and cat food, not to mention the grains used for bird food. The pet food business is a billion-dollar business in America, considerably less in most other nations, but still a large potential for that day when the human population of the world will need every calorie.

Such inefficiencies in the food chain might be alleviated by raising double-duty animals, as pets destined ultimately for food. However, such an approach raises the hackles of many who would find it impossible to make a feast on rabbits, chickens, and some other animals that become family pets although primarily raised for food.

Pets aside, there is a far more serious question with respect to animals in general that we should look into before proceeding with our examination of meat as food for the world. It would seem that if we were to eliminate or phase out animal life, we could make it possible for five times as many more humans to live on the presently cultivated land of the world. For a number of reasons, the solution to the food problem is not that simple.

High on the Hog

Recalling the hunting and gathering period, we realize that
primitive man may have eaten much "higher on the hog" than
the average human of today. In early times man subsisted to a
large extent on his hunting spoils, and meat was standard fare.
When human numbers or food shortages led to the development
of agriculture, the result was less animal flesh to go around, in
spite of the domestication of those creatures man had once stalked
for game.

Now, it *is* possible to have a fairly balanced diet, with ample
amounts of each of the necessary amino acids, using only plants.
Although there is perhaps no one plant that has all the amino
acids, a mixture of various plants will provide them. The efficacy
of even one kind of plant is described in the Bible:

Then said Daniel to Melzar . . .
Prove thy servants, I beseech thee, ten days; and let them give us
pulse to eat, and water to drink.
Then let our countenances be looked upon before thee, and the
countenance of the children that eat of the portion of the king's
meat: . . .
And at the end of ten days their countenances appeared fairer and
fatter in flesh than all of the children which did eat the portion of the
king's meat.

Daniel 1:11–15

Vegetarianism is practiced today by great numbers of people,
perhaps involuntarily in most cases. Certain Hindu and Buddhist
sects can rationalize their lack of meat on religious grounds; there
are other religions, including the Seventh-Day Adventists, whose
members eat no flesh. Roman Catholics until recently abstained
from all meat but fish on Friday. But beginning in about the middle of the last century vegetarianism became popular among some
for other reasons, including humane (a desire to harm no living
creature) and hygienic (a fear of disease). Some vegetarians shun

all flesh, some permit the eating of netted fish. The Jewish refusal to eat meat from cloven-footed animals stems from hygienic
concern, although the practice was woven into religious tradition.
Advancing meat prices tend to create groups of neovegetarians.
However, most of those who eat no meat or little meat do not
have a choice—except to eat plants or starve!

The Need for Meat

Animal protein is "high-quality" protein, protein that is bio-
logically better than that found in plants. This is, of course, not
accident or coincidence, since man is an animal and requires the
same amino acids for the living processes as do the lower animals.
Animal protein, then, is rich in lysine, histidine, tryptophan,
methionine, threonine, leucine, valine, and phenylalanine—all important amino acids.

While few of us are qualified nutritionists from the standpoint
of formal education, the human body generally knows and craves
what it needs. Our tastes and preferences have deep physiological
roots; they are usually looking out for our bodily needs—although
it is difficult to know why we crave sweets in the quantities most
of us do!

Forget for the moment the monotony and blandness of a vegetable diet day in and year out. There are other shortcomings,
principally from a nutritional standpoint. Meat, milk, eggs, and
fish protein are considered of high quality because they contain
a balance of the eight vital amino acids our bodies need; present
plant proteins are lacking in one or more of these. Further, those
people forced to subsist on a diet mainly of corn, rice, or wheat
are likely to be shortchanged with respect to lysine, tryptophan,
or methionine. Even the pulses, or legumes, Daniel wrote of fall
somewhat short, despite their oilseed richness. Soybeans lack
methionine, cottonseed is low in lysine and threonine, and peanuts
are deficient in methionine, lysine, and tryptophan.

154   THE GEOMETRY OF HUNGER

Can We Afford Meat?

The farm animal industry accounts for more than half the income of the American farmer, yet meat and other high-protein meat products account for only about 10 percent of our diet in the United States. Some fortunate people eat meat almost exclusively. According to nutritionists, all people should have an appreciable amount of their food in the form of meat protein, since, as we have seen, it fulfills our needs more completely. Unfortunately, most of the world is less well off than America and many other more advanced societies; the law of "ecological tithes" prevents them from having as much meat, milk, and eggs as they should have.

Meat products represent a large share of the food on United States tables. But to provide that quantity of nourishment we have to feed the animals that produce the meat something like ten times that weight of feed. This seems like skimming the cream off the food supply, and to some extent it is. The "have" nations tend to be choosy and even wasteful in their diets. The "have-nots" cannot be either, and few of them can afford to put ten pounds of grain into a cow to get one pound of meat, even though that one pound of meat is a very superior food.

There are several inherent disadvantages to using meat for food: (1) It can't be produced as efficiently as grain; (2) animals compete with man for food; (3) there is more disease risk in animals than in plants; (4) animal production may compete with other food production for land use; and (5) meat, milk, and eggs are not as easy to store as plants, particularly the grains.

All these arguments seem to favor vegetarianism. If we have the equivalent of 15 billion humans eating ten times as much food as they give back maybe we *had* better declare open season on our competitors the animals. However, the Scientific Advisory Committee panel on the world food problem has drawn a bead on these false beliefs about animal food production in its 1967 "Report on the World Food Problem."

The unique and important contribution that animals can make to the world food supply is often underestimated or overlooked by world food planners, presumably because of the belief that increases in animal production can be made only by diverting to animals, foods that otherwise would be eaten by people. This approach ignores the fact that livestock consume great quantities of food such as forages, wastes, by-products, and even urea that cannot be eaten by man. Whether or not grains are fed to livestock is generally a question of economics. When it is profitable to do so, livestock producers feed grains; when it is not, they utilize other feedstuffs.

In the opinion of the Subpanel, as well as other knowledgeable experts, providing adequate quantities of animal products is one of the most effective ways to improve world protein nutrition.

Tithing Pays

Let's consider these points. Those who object to raising animals for meat as inefficient forget or are unaware that animals can scavenge and make use of feeds unusable for anything else. Also, some 60 percent of the world's agricultural land is non-arable; it is good only for grazing. Animals are the only practical means of using this vast food resource.

If we humans were to be "pastured" on a western desert range-land and expected to survive, we would fail miserably and soon starve to death—this in spite of billions upon billions of calories all around us in the grass and other vegetation. We can make no use of most of this because we are not ruminants. Cows are, because they have four stomachs and can progressively process roughage from the pasture or elsewhere into protein in solid or liquid form. Our own stomachs are designed for more refined foods, just as high-powered and delicately tuned automobiles require high-test gas and cannot run on wood or coal or old newspapers as a primitive steam engine could.

Even in the United States, where it is complained that valuable grains are fed to them, livestock consume from 60 to 90 percent forage in their diets. The introduction of livestock to Florida, where they were fed grapefruit wastes, is an example of efficient scavenging. Animals also can live on nonprotein nitrogen in the form of urea and convert it to protein; cows fed urea as a sole source of protein have been good producers.

N. W. Pirie has made an interesting suggestion in this regard. Noting that the camel seems able to conserve urea, and that urea can be fed to cattle to provide nitrogen necessary in the diet, he suggests that animal geneticists select cattle that are able to secrete urea from the bloodstream through the rumen wall rather than excreting it through the kidney. This would save part of the nitrogen wasted in urine.

Other wastes and by-products that can be fed to meat animals include residues from corn, rice, wheat, sorghums, oats and barley, sugar beets and cane, cottonseed meal, gin wastes, brewery grain residues, molasses, meat scraps, fat, tankage, bone meal and manures, fruit-processing residues, and such oilseeds as peanuts, safflowers, soybeans, sesame seeds, palm, and coconut meal.

The Sacred Cow

The introduction of mechanized equipment on farms and ranches has resulted in a sharp drop in the number of horses and mules needed for draft purposes. However, since in less-developed countries it is slow and expensive to convert from animal power to gasoline or diesel engines, in many parts of the world the animal still plays a major role as a source of power on the farm. This is one of the reasons for the seemingly disproportionate share of livestock in undeveloped countries. A former Viceroy of India has stated that "the cow and the working bullock bear on their patient backs the whole structure of Indian agriculture." This situation prevails not only in India and Pakistan, but the Far East, the Near East, Africa, and Latin America.

Bullocks supply most of the draft animal power in India, with

India's controversial "sacred cow," while little used for food, does provide much of the motive power for agriculture and other tasks.
The Rockefeller Foundation

cow dung providing the main cooking fuel and being of great importance as an organic fertilizer. The sacred cows also supply milk. The cattle are partly scavengers, obtaining the bulk of their food from roadsides, ditches, and agricultural wastes. Draft animals, and those that are raised for wool, mohair, and other fibers, provide further bonuses in that some are eventually eaten. In the meantime, they produce economically important fibers, plus, in the case of cattle, buffalo, and goats, milk.

Marvin Harris, in his book, *The Myth of the Sacred Cow*, debunks the claims of those who say India should eliminate its cows. According to Harris, the cow is a vital link in the food chain and is needed for its work output rather than as a direct food. He quotes Gandhi's remark that the cows are sacred because they are needed. The Hindu doctrine of *ahinsa* restricts slaughter of cattle, but in parts of India cows *are* slaughtered. Pagans, Christians,

Moslems and even some Hindus eat beef. There are 175 million head of cattle in India. Castration of bulls is being practiced to some extent, and IUD loops are being experimented with in cows!

The tractor and the other mechanized equipment of the developed countries is coming slowly, but for many years draft animals will continue to be needed in the countries named above. Since their main competitor is man himself, killing off animals to save food would be shortsighted as a solution and would make farming even harder for those people who depend on it most.

One Man's Meat

It is possible to supplement food grains with additives in the form of needed proteins, an idea that has been carried out with a number of prepared products. But these have generally gone over like lead balloons with the people who need them most. Strong preferences in food have been built up over the centuries, and these tastes cannot be readily changed. Difficult as it is for the vegetarian to accept, the best way to provide proteins for malnourished millions around the world is with meat, eggs, milk, and cheese. Most of these are acceptable, not only to the amino-craving body of the human organism, but to the dietary and cultural heritage of the hungry.

If meat products are the best food for proteins, it is reasonable that nations produce as much meat as they can, depending on available land, economics, and so on. A few samples will bear out this point. Japan is one of the most densely populated countries in the world, with more than seven people dependent on each acre of farm land. Not surprisingly, the Japanese rank at the bottom of the list in the number of farm animals per human. Japan, however, is increasing her animal population and at the same time learning how to make it more productive of animal protein for human consumption. In the last twenty years, for example, milk production has been increased by 400 percent.

For every ten Japanese there are only six livestock. In the United

States instead of one-seventh of an acre of tilled land per person, there are more than two and one-half acres per person, and there are about six livestock for each person. Australia has almost six acres of tilled land and about thirty-eight livestock per person!

Potatoes and beans are obviously cheaper than top sirloin, or even hamburger and hot dogs. Economic pressure could conceivably shift our diet more toward plants and away from meat protein, but it is increasing population that will be more likely to do it. With a population of 500 million in the United States we might not be able to feed sufficient livestock and might have to eat more vegetables, with cereal for breakfast instead of ham and eggs.

Meat is the key to the world food problem. In 1967 the President's Science Advisory Committee reported that

. . . there is no world-wide shortage of food in terms of quantity (calories) or quality (protein) at the moment. But in the developing countries, where two-thirds of the world's population live, there is overwhelming clinical evidence of under-nutrition (too few calories) and malnutrition (particularly, lack of protein) among the people. Clearly, millions of individuals are *not* receiving the amounts of food suggested by average figures.

People Need Protein

In the decade between 1954 and 1964, according to the Food and Agriculture Organization, world production of protein more than matched population growth; in fact, the average daily supply increased by 7.5 percent. This increase was not uniform around the world, however, and Latin America, with a meager 0.4 percent increase, just about kept even. Oceania increased by 1.1 percent, but its protein ration was already quite high. North America jumped 4.9 percent, the Far East by a healthy 14.7 percent, Europe by 16.2 percent, and the Near East by a whopping 25.9 percent.

Despite these glowing statistics there remains a very serious protein problem, a problem painfully obvious in the malnourished millions of the world, thousands of whom starve each day. The Scientific Advisory Committee's food panel reported that there is no shortage of animal protein in the world as a whole; taken as an average enough animal protein is produced to give each of us about twenty grams. However, supplies available in the developing countries amount to only nine grams per person per day compared to forty grams or more in the developed countries.

Argentina consumes the most meat protein, some forty-seven grams per person per day. Australia and New Zealand are next, with about forty grams. Next is the United States at about thirty-six grams; then Canada at thirty-three; Denmark, Ireland, and Switzerland with about twenty-two; Sweden twenty; and Finland fifteen grams. Supplementing with milk and fish brings these countries to as high as seventy-five grams of animal protein per day. In contrast, developing countries like India, Peru, the Philippines, China, and Turkey get only about five grams of meat and a total of not more than fifteen grams, even with milk and fish added.

The Food and Agriculture Organization's short-term target for animal protein supplies for the developing countries is fifteen grams, and the long-term target is twenty-one grams per person per day. The FAO believes these targets could be realized if maximum use were made of "all available resources." This is a tall order.

Lead a Horse to Water

Cows are sacred in India, but worldwide more beef is eaten than any other meat. Just about 50 percent of the total comes from cattle; 41 percent is pork; 8 percent is lamb, mutton, and goat. And, while it must be a blow to another kind of lover of horseflesh, 1 percent of the world's meat is horsemeat. Milk accounts for more weight in proteins than meat. And poultry and eggs together represent perhaps 10 percent of the world consumption of protein.

Of the estimated 6 billion livestock and fowl in the world, 60 percent are in the underdeveloped countries. Yet these countries produce only 20 to 30 percent of the world's meat, milk, and eggs. Why this disappointing disparity, which results in a proportionate shortage to the developing countries in consumption of animal protein? It is because those countries fail to make use of scientific knowledge and technological processes to control disease and to increase production.

The Food and Agriculture Organization sets as a realistic goal the reduction of losses from disease by as much as 50 percent, and an increase in production of animal protein of about 25 percent. But many countries simply let cattle fend for themselves. Sometimes they are powerless to do more, for diseases continue to plague animals in developing lands, a long catalog of woes including rinderpest, bovine pleuropneumonia, foot-and-mouth disease, African horse sickness, swine fever, hog cholera, Newcastle disease, trypanosomiasis, East Coast fever, and fowl plague.

Range and pasture management techniques practiced successfully in the developed countries must be adopted and adapted to increase meat production in the developing countries. It is of little use to increase the size of herds if there is not proper and sufficient feed available for the animals. While animals can make use of a great many agricultural and industrial wastes, many developing countries lack such wastes or the knowledge of how to use them properly. Others, such as Peru, export such products as fish meal instead of using it to fatten their own animals and poultry.

Howard T. Odum, in his book *Power and Survival*, outlines a Ugandan cattle-keeping system. In it, only 11 percent of the land is under cultivation and the cattle consume only 18 percent of range plant production. To attempt to increase this exploitation would be costly in capital investment, and would also risk overgrazing and upsetting the soil bases. Such a system yields to the men tending it the pitifully small protein total of 0.06 percent of the amount consumed by the cattle! It is, of course, better than no meat at all.

A big part of the problem of low productivity of livestock stems from ignorance of even the most basic facts of animal life by primitive husbandmen. Examples are cited by experts at the University of Arizona in Tucson. Called in by Indian agents to help with food supplements for cattle, the agriculturists at once suggested salt. "Forget salt," they were told. "The Indians say the cows eat it up as fast as they put it out!" And Brazilian officials, well-meaning but ignorant of animal husbandry, make it nearly impossible to thin out old, sick, and nonproductive animals —because that would waste meat. With such a lack of understanding of the economics of food production, it is difficult to make much improvement. Thus education continues to be a big part of the problem.

The United States, with an already efficient animal husbandry, has further increased yields for the last decade by about 2 percent a year. For example, feeding Aureomycin, Terramycin and penicillin to cattle, hogs, and chickens has been found to produce more rapid growth, and the antibiotics control systemic bacteria and even fungus diseases as well.

In many developing lands advisers find that cattle-raisers, far from being ready for such techniques, have little knowledge even of such fundamentals as the reproductive cycle and basic breeding techniques. In the United States a cow is fattened to about 1,000 pounds in two years. In developing lands it may take five or six years to produce livestock weighing only 600 pounds. Calf crops approximate 80 percent and more in the United States, but only 50 percent at best in the tropics and other developing areas. Besides, ignorance, custom, tradition, social and religious beliefs, and political ideas all hinder the adoption of modern cattle-breeding techniques. The traditional bridal dowry of cattle, for example, is one reason for the inefficient overstocking of grazing lands in much of Africa and Asia. Another tradition keeps herds large so that when epidemic strikes there will be a better chance of survivors to enable the herd to be started again.

It is estimated that there are about 165,000 veterinarians

Results of scientific feeding of hogs in Colombia. Animal on left was fed common corn; center hog was fed genetically improved corn; the hog labeled MS flourished on a protein-corn diet supplemented with soybean meal.
The Rockefeller Foundation

throughout the world; however, only 17,000 of these live in the areas needing them most. The situation is even worse with respect to geneticists, physiologists, land management experts, and nutritionists. Again, tradition is hard to buck. It is difficult for some cattle-raisers to believe that there is more to the business than their ancestors passed on to them. Nevertheless, some progress is being made in spite of all the difficulties, and there are encouraging signs. Breeding of new cattle strains such as Brahman, Santa Gertrudis, Nandi, and Boran, has been successful for the tropics. Where modern methods of animal husbandry and sound principles of disease control have been adopted, efficient livestock production has been achieved even in Kenya, Rhodesia, Australia, and the Republic of South Africa. There are hundreds of fine herds in these countries, despite the fact that some are tropical lands, with the problems of heat and disease that make the mainte- nance of productive livestock hazardous. This is particularly en- couraging because Africa has more land area per human and per head of livestock than any area except Australia and New Zea- land.

Poultry Is Protein

Man has for thousands of years made use of the high-quality protein in birds, ducks, chickens, turkeys, and other feathered creatures, including eggs. Modern science has moved toward chickens capable of laying an egg a day, far more than the output of the lazy ancestors of these fowl. And the mass production of broilers in what amount to completely automated meat factories is one of the brightest developments in the protein field. Mexico, a late starter in the poultry industry, began commercial egg pro- duction only in 1954, but today the hen crops approach 20 million. In 1958 that country got into the commercial broiler in- dustry, and by 1966 was marketing 25 million broilers. Other na- tions involved in poultry include Venezuela, Peru—whose fish catch could provide all the needed feed—Pakistan, Java, and Nigeria.

More Meat for the Table

> But mice and rats and such small deer
> Have been Tom's food for seven long year.
> William Shakespeare, *King Lear*

There are many thousands of kinds of animals, and men have sampled the flesh of a goodly number of these down through the ages. In times of famine people have eaten rats and worse; college boys used to bolt down goldfish for kicks. In various parts of the world some people still eat termites and other ants—chocolate-

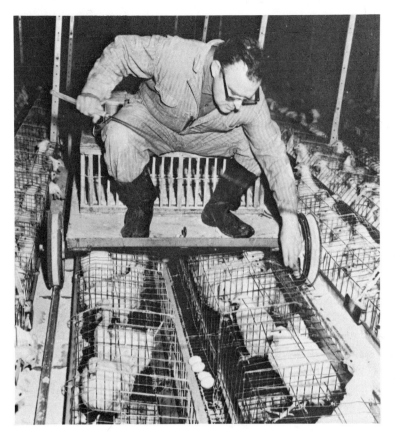

Inspector on rolling platform checks chickens in high-rise "egg factory."
USDA

covered or plain—larvae, snakes, lizards, crickets, water beetle eggs, locusts, and even cockroaches, plus, among other foods, lion, hippo, and elephant meat. But by and large man has settled on a relatively few of the animal species for food, just as he has done in the plant department.

One obvious possibility for providing more meat for the tables of those who are short of protein is to exploit species of animals not now in general use—India, of course, being perhaps unfairly criticized for not using its sacred cows for meat, thus ending the waste of the feed they consume. However, Australia abounds in kangaroos, and "roo" meat is eaten by some. And at one time, as we have seen, jackrabbits nearly overran Australia. Jackrabbit is protein, and does not necessarily compete with man for the food it thrives on.

There are doubtless many more creatures that would make fine eating, like the eland, a large antelope touted by many as a good bet. Pirie suggests the capybara, a hefty South American rodent. Completely aquatic and noncompetitive with other animals for food, it is said to be palatable. So too are the manatee (once taken for mermaids by homesick sailors) and the dugong. These creatures could also control aquatic weeds while they were at it. The Scientific Advisory Committee recommends more study of other wild animals, particularly marine mammals, as meat-producers.

Although wild animals contribute to a large extent to the diet in many lands—a good example being Africa, richly endowed with a variety of wildlife, much of which is a good source of food and is dietetically acceptable to African palates—it has been impossible to measure adequately the amounts of such game taken and brought to the table.

Studies in Africa, Australia, the Soviet Union, the United States, and the United Kingdom indicate that wild animals yield more meat in some areas than livestock. In other areas, a mixing of domestic and wild species is more efficient. Results in Africa indicate that it may be unwise to decimate herds of wild animals in attempts to wipe out disease and protect livestock. For example, a fifty-square-mile area that was carefully monitored was found to contain sixteen species of grazing and browsing animals, with a population of seventy-six animals per mile and a standing crop of 19,000 pounds. The minimum annual crop was harvested by shooting and sold commercially as meat. Some 118,000 pounds of meat were produced. To convert the area to conventional livestock production would have resulted in an annual yield of 95,000 pounds of meat and a profit of only one-sixth as much money.

While game taken by hunters is important in some localities, it represents only a tiny portion of total meat supply. *USDA*

Another important factor in the use of wild animals in lands like Africa is their resistance to disease, through ages of subsisting in such an environment.

Man has a cultural and physiological heritage as a meat-eater. Far from a luxury, meat is a highly necessary food that is rich in essential proteins. Processed by our meat animals, it is high-quality fare, the cream of the food crop. For these reasons a high priority has been put on meat production by those concerned with global food problems. Fortunately, there is an excellent supplement for meat, and we consider next the prospects of food from our oceans, rivers, and lakes.

There is the green pasture where our children's grandchildren will go for bread.
Herman Melville, *Moby Dick*

CHAPTER 9

Ocean Harvest

In response to talk of the shortage of meat and the protein gap, there are those who say, "Let 'em eat fish." This is a logical suggestion, and the chances are good that we will further exploit that "animal that resides in the water," as Samuel Johnson defined fish in his dictionary. How far-reaching a sea change will take place in our diet remains to be seen.

Much has been written and said about the new "green granaries"; of how man will farm the sea much as he does the land, with cowboys (perhaps "dolphinboys" would be more appropriate) riding their undersea ranges and food being harvested from seaweeds that grow in bountiful profusion hundreds of feet long. Algae, the green scum that plagues ponds and swimming pools, will be cultivated to provide appealing and nourishing new food. Man will return to the sea, poetically, for sustenance the land he invaded is beginning to deny him.

There are other writers who protest this concept as so much bilge water. Borgstrom is one expert who deplores the "loose talk" of feeding fish to the world's hungry. While it is true that fisheries have made a dramatic doubling of the ocean catch in a recent decade, it is just as true that fish still provide only about 2 percent of the calories consumed by the world. Thus if the catch could miraculously be doubled again in a single year it would add only 2 percent to the total food basket.

The truth of the sea's promise lies somewhere between extreme views, although perhaps closer to that of the pessimists. Just how much greater catch can be harvested ranges from Borgstrom's belief that we couldn't take much more from the sea than we did in 1964 (we have *already* increased that by close to 100 percent, however) to estimates by other authorities of thirtyfold increases in the foreseeable future.

Angling History

Fishing is as old as hunting, and love of the sport was deeply ingrained in man long before Izaak Walton wrote his inspired lines for and about the angler. Witness how many of us, like him, have "laid aside business and gone a-fishing." Fishing is as atavistic a pursuit as hunting or congregating around the campfire in the evening.

The first fish were probably taken by hand, and then with crude clubs. The spear, a later refinement, is still used today, and arrows were also found to be effective. Copper hooks dating to 2800 B.C. have been discovered; stone and bone hooks may go back to as long as 10,000 years ago. In fact, bone "gorges" are thought to have been in use for as long as 30,000 or 40,000 years! A gorge is a straight splinter of bone, sharpened at each end and so tied to the fishing line that it is swallowed by the fish with bait and then turns sidewise to lodge in the gullet. Gorges are still used by some fishermen, and the Japanese continue to train cormorants to dive for fish, as they have for centuries. The net, too, seems to have been one of man's earliest inventions; he began to weave them soon after the spinning and weaving of fibers came about. Nets were in existence in the ancient civilizations of Sumer and China, probably antedating writing.

A fishing boat working off the coast near Valparaiso. Pelicans swarm up to the nets to catch the fish—mostly hake—which slip through the holes.
FAO photo by S. Larrain

How seriously the "compleat angler" takes his love makes an interesting and ironic point. Although fish ranks as the most important wildlife from an economic standpoint, and the world commercial harvest is something over 65 million tons a year, about 20 million sport fishermen in the United States alone spend over $2 billion a year on the sport—more than the gross value of the world commercial catch! It is obvious that much catfish at twenty dollars a pound is eaten, perhaps more than equally priced deer and quail. The sport-fishing catch in the United States is something over 600 million pounds; about three pounds for each of us—assuming it is all cleaned and eaten.

The Fisheries Today

One definition of fish is "any aquatic vertebrate with fins instead of legs." Fish appeared early in evolution and were the only vertebrates until the late Devonian period. There remain some 30,000 living species, and in addition there are mollusks, such as oysters and clams, and crustaceans, including crabs, shrimp, and lobsters, that are of commercial value as food. As he does with plants, man uses only a few dozen of the fish, and proportionately less of the mollusks and crustaceans.

The northeastern Atlantic yields halibut, flounder, cod, haddock, coalfish, herring, and shrimp; the northwestern Pacific salmon, flatfish, herring, crab, shrimp, lobster, squid, and octopus. The northwestern Atlantic has the same as the northeastern, plus lobster. The Indo-Pacific provides herring, bonito, mackerel, and shrimp; Asia's fresh water the ayu, salmon, milkfish, and carp. Russian fresh water yields salmon and whitefish, Africa a variety of fish, and northern North America trout, whitefish, bass, and perch and its relatives.

Fish, like meat, is an excellent source of protein, and it does provide about 20 percent of the animal protein consumed. This proportion is not uniform around the world, of course. In the United States only 5 to 10 percent of our animal protein comes from seafood. We eat about ten or eleven pounds per person per year, an amount that has remained remarkably constant for more than half a century. The Swiss just about match our fish consumption; the British, with their affection for fish and chips, double that amount. Spaniards consume more than thirty pounds per head per year, and the neighboring Portuguese about fifty pounds, slightly more than the Swedes and Danes, who are traditionally a fish-eating people. But it is in Asia that seafood is indispensable. The fish market in Tokyo is the largest in the world, and each day sells some 4 million pounds of fresh fish.

In 1968 the Japanese people averaged sixty-one pounds of fish each, six times the consumption in the United States.

It is said that a modern freighter load of codfish could feed 35,000 people for a year, but there are some countries that make no use, or very little use, of fish. Peru is cited as the classic example, exporting practically all of its huge fish catch—as fish meal to feed chickens and pigs.

Fish is probably not brain food and fish dinners may not make us all "spring like a flea," as Thomas Jordan put it. However, beyond being just protein of high quality, fish is thought to guard against heart disease. This ailment kills 500,000 in the United States yearly, and many nutritionists claim that this toll could be cut appreciably if we ate more fish.

The foregoing paragraph, incidentally, should point out the frustrating complexity of the food-population problem. If we eat more fish and save more lives, there will be that many more mouths to feed, of course. And that many more people to reproduce more children, and so on ad infinitum. In fact, Dr. John Arbuthnot, Scottish physician to royalty, some 250 years ago wrote the following commentary on fish as a breeder of men: ". . . a Diet of Fish is more rich and alkalescent than that of Flesh, and therefore very improper for such as practice Mortification. The Inhabitants of Sea-Port Towns are generally prolifick." Whether or not statistics would bear out Arbuthnot's charge is questionable, but perhaps there is at least food for thought in the notion.

In the United States the fish catch has remained as stable as our consumption—for the last thirty years commercial fishermen have brought in about six billion pounds of fish annually. Since population has increased considerably in that time, we must import more fish to make up the difference. It is interesting, too, that while there were about 160,000 commercial fishermen in this country in 1950, the figure now is less than 135,000. There are good reasons for this, beyond the fact that modern techniques are more efficient.

John Chalkhill's "The Angler" rhapsodizes over the fishing life
in this manner:

> Oh the gallant fisher's life!
> It is the best of any;
> 'Tis full of pleasure, void of strife,
> And 'tis beloved by many.

Scott put it less poetically but more truthfully when he said,
"It's no fish you're buying, it's men's lives." For fishing ranks as
more dangerous than mining and is a far lonelier life, with the
crew often away from home and family for months at a time.

While the United States has not accelerated its fishing, the
rest of the world has. In fact, in the last two decades the fish
catch increased faster than population, and from 1956 to 1966 it
nearly doubled. Presently the catch is about 130 billion pounds
of fish a year, most of it taken by hook or net. The most remarkable change in fishing has been the growth of the catch in
waters of the Southern Hemisphere. Prior to 1950 perhaps not
more than 5 percent of the total came from below the Equator;
but today southern waters account for about 35 percent. Peru
is responsible for this surprising change, with its anchovy fishing
in the rich upwelling from the Humboldt current off its shores.

The Green Granaries

If it is difficult to the point of impossibility to get Americans
to eat more fish, even with the idea of avoiding heart trouble, and
if Peruvians seem to prefer malnutrition to eating fish, the prospects of greatly increasing our exploitation of the green granaries
would seem about as remote as farming the moon. However,
Peru's fish meal makes its way indirectly into our protein-craving
tissues in a manner we shall discuss shortly. Assuming that ways
will be found to make use of any increase in the sea harvest, let's
turn our attention to the problems attending such increases.

It is difficult to understand why the sea, representing more than twice as much area as the land surface of earth, yields only 2 percent of our needs. Why can't we get *twice* as much food from the sea as from the land? Some optimists think we can, but they are outnumbered by more realistic experts on such matters. These latter point out some basic biological facts to document their case.

For one thing, the sea generally is not nearly so productive per acre as is land, as noted earlier, there are "wet deserts," and some of these are more barren than the worst dry deserts. While it is true that there is ample carbon dioxide in the oceans, ranging from 0.05 gram assimilated per square meter per day in the "barren" blue Mediterranean and the Sargasso Sea, to ten times that amount in temperate and colder seas, there is little nitrogen in water. Nitrogen is important to the production of plant matter, and, while in rich fertile soil there may be as much as 0.5 percent of it, unpolluted seawater contains a maximum of only 0.00005 percent nitrogen. The ratio of plant productivity does not work out as badly as this difference would indicate; however, while rich topsoil can be made to produce up to 200 tons of dry organic matter a year per acre, an acre of rich ocean water yields only about 20 tons.

To the argument that instead of a few inches or feet of soil the sea represents a depth of thousands of productive feet, the facts are that more than 80 percent of the life in the sea is found in the top 600 feet or so. Between 600 feet and 10,000 feet there is about 16 percent, and only about 1 percent of all sea life is found below 10,000 feet. For this reason some authorities believe the sea produces only about twice as much plant material as does the land. More importantly, most of this plant life is unavailable to us as food, even for animal feed, if we wanted to use it indirectly.

Many have suggested that we eat plankton, going to the primary source of energy in the sea rather than wasting it through all the long food chain. However, there seems little hope of doing

Researcher brings up net
of plankton, the basis of
the marine food chain.
This picture was taken on
the research vessel *Sis-
cowet* on Lake Superior.
*Bureau of Commercial Fish-
eries*

this. The reason is the same one that prevents the economical
extraction of gold from seawater: even though that precious
mineral is there to the value of billions of dollars, it costs more to
process the gold—and the plankton—than either is worth. A cubic
yard of water yields about three-thousandths of an ounce of tiny
plankton, and it would be necessary to filter a million gallons of
water to get a pound of the stuff if it *could* be filtered, and only a
few brave men have suggested such schemes. By the time you
have handled a million gallons of water for one pound of marine
life, there had better be a pearl or at least some ambergris included in the catch or the operation loses money.

There is one faint possibility in concentrating on areas of the
sea that teem with certain kinds of plankton, such as the Ant-
arctic krill, a food preferred by some whales. Krill are shrimp,
about the size of commercial varieties, and hardly the plankton

we generally think of. A whale cruises through the water inhaling krill and consuming up to three tons of it in a day. Unfortunately the sea is not thick with krill except in certain places—which only whales seem able to find with any degree of assurance. Even could we find krill and as efficiently extract them from the water, there are so many more humans than whales that each of us might get only a taste.

On land we tolerate the conversion loss in our meat-producing animals so we can have high protein and tasty food. But we also eat nine pounds of corn or other grains and vegetables for each pound of meat. And from the sea all we can get is the meat. If we were faced with twice as many mouths to feed as we now have, and could not boost production of food on land, we would then have to increase our sea harvest about fiftyfold to do the job. It doesn't seem likely that we can do that.

There is a food pyramid in the sea as well as on land, as we saw in a previous chapter. George Borgstrom discouragingly points out how it works: 500 pounds of phytoplankton (plant plankton) produces 100 pounds of zooplankton (animal plankton); 100 pounds of zooplankton makes 10 of herring, which in turn makes 1 of mackerel. And this makes only 1.6 ounces of tuna. One pound of tuna takes 5,000 pounds of phytoplankton; 1 pound of codfish takes 50,000 pounds of phytoplankton. The law of tithes, marine style, works even more disadvantageously than that on land.

Borgstrom also points out that there are few aquatic counterparts of ruminants like cows and sheep. Only those species like sardines and menhaden, he claims, qualify in this respect. The herring, sometimes called "the hog of the sea," Borgstrom says is misnamed, more resembling the anteater, which eats insects that subsist on plants. With the observation that the fish catch represents the end result of a plant base between sixty and seventy times the weight of the world's wheat crop, Borgstrom concludes that we have about reached the limits of nature's productivity in the sea.

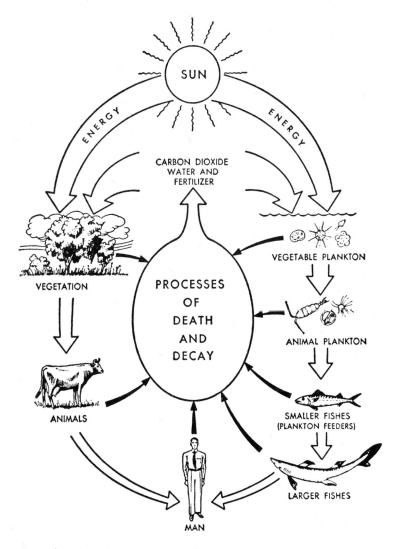

The food chain in the sea is longer and more complex than that on land.

Reproduced by permission of Charles Scribner's Sons from The Sun, the Sea, and Tomorrow *by Henry Chapin and F. G. Walton Smith. Copyright 1954 Charles Scribner's Sons*

The Optimists

Despite such sobering facts of sea life, there are many who
agree with the Nantucket folk who looked toward the green pastures seaward. Gilbert and Sullivan expressed an obvious truth in
the lines from *Patience:* "There's fish in the sea, no doubt of it,/As
good as ever came out of it." Just two years after Gilbert penned
these lines in 1881, a more scientific Englishman named T. H.
Huxley observed: "I believe that the cod fishery, the herring
fishery, the pilchard fishery, the mackerel fishery, and probably
all the great fisheries are inexhaustible; that is to say that nothing
we do seriously affects the number of the fish." Chances are
Huxley would modify his belief in light of today's whopping
catches. But he might still join a number of other scientists who
foresee a sizable increase in fish harvest yet to come.

In 1962 H. W. Graham and R. L. Edwards estimated 6 billion
acres of continental-shelf fisheries acreage, and a potential catch
of 55 million metric tons. By 1964, 56 million tons had been
caught, and this has since increased to 65 million tons. Graham
and Edwards then upped their estimate to 115 million tons. Other
estimates of the potential sea harvest range up to 2 *billion* tons
annually, and two sources have made that bountiful prediction.
This would be about a thirtyfold increase in food taken from the
sea. Such optimistic estimates assume an annual net production in
sea plants of up to 19 billion tons of carbon and a total weight
of 500 billion tons of phytoplankton, the floating marine plants
that are the primary source of seafood energy. Two billion tons
of fish then represents an efficiency of only 0.04 percent in the
many-level food pyramid of the sea.

From about 1955 the sea harvest has increased some 7 percent
a year. At this rate, it would take about fifty years to reach the
2-billion-ton bonanza suggested. The Scientific Advisory Board
cautiously suggests increases of from double the present catch to

perhaps 500 million tons or more, an eightfold increase, and surely worth angling for.

Improvements in Fishing

There are primitive "subsistence" fishermen today who may land only a thousand pounds of fish a year. Scientific and technical developments make it possible for their counterparts on a modern trawler to bring in 400,000 pounds per man in the same length of time. For example, an experimental trawler operated by the U.S. Bureau of Commercial Fisheries off the coast of Washington used radar gear to trawl at 300 feet and netted 42,000 pounds of hake in *one hour*.

Thus far the techniques of fishing with electric shock weapons, lights, and magnetic fields to disorient the prey, and pumps to suck them into the boat, have not proved as effective as improvements in the time-tried nets and hooks. A breakthrough in some of these more sophisticated methods could provide the quantum jump in fishing, however.

Fishing practices are probably as important as techniques. Overfishing is harmful, as has been demonstrated in the drastic reduction in the numbers of whales in global waters. A single large blue whale is worth $5,000 and more in meat, oil, bone, vitamins, hormones, and other pharmaceutical chemicals, and even provides ambergris for perfume-making on occasion. But greediness on the part of whalers may be wiping out the whales, an object lesson in trying to extract too much from the golden sea we might well heed. George Borgstrom points out that the manatee is already about gone, and the green turtle is on the way out.

Underfishing is wasteful, too. The catch from rivers and lakes ranges from 5 to 175 pounds per acre a year, with about a 20-pound average. In overflow swamps, such as the great rivers of Asia and Africa, the range is 30 to 400 pounds per acre and about 100 pounds average. In reservoirs the catch is 5 to 100 pounds, with an average of 25 pounds. It is estimated that more intensive fishing could probably increase this freshwater catch by 50 to 100 percent.

Sport fishing has delayed the commercial catching of hake and anchovies off the West Coast, since they are good sport fish. But in 1966 an arrangement was made with the California Fish and Game Commission to allow 150 million pounds to be harvested for fish meal and oil. Anchovies should support a million-ton catch a year off California, and jack mackerel could be greatly increased from the 45,000 tons in a recent year. The United States could also increase its catches of demersal (bottom) fish in the Bering Sea and Gulf of Alaska, as well as ocean perch in the latter; Russia and Japan are catching more than a million tons a year of these. Indian Ocean research shows much unused tuna, shrimp, lobster, and sardines.

Some writers believe that elimination of predators of food fish might raise production appreciably. One particular species of starfish eats half the plaice in the North Sea. The possibility of chemically poisoning them has been suggested, much as we now use pesticides to rid our land crops and animals from harmful pests.

Pollution

Nature provides plenty of competitors and predators to reduce man's take-home harvest from the sea, at times polluting the water with a "red tide" of marine protozoa that kill fish and other living things in the sea on a large scale. At other times algae bloom so profusely that they, too, become a menace. While some claim that man is responsible for the red tide, such phenomena existed long before phosphates and other chemicals that are thought to do the damage. The *Iliad* describes the red tide, and so does the Bible:

Thus saith the Lord, In this thou shalt know that I am the Lord: behold, I will smite with the rod that is in mine hand upon the waters which are in the river, and they shall be turned to blood.

Diver brings up one of more than 14,000 abalones relocated to make room for breakwater for nuclear power plant near Diablo Canyon in California.
Pacific Gas & Electric Company

And the fish that is in the river shall die, and the river shall stink; and the Egyptians shall loathe to drink of the water of the river.

Man has established himself as a polluter on the grand scale, however. The tragic example of pollution in Lake Erie is repeated on a lesser scale in other lakes, rivers, and even the oceans of the world. Oil from on shore, and from ships and undersea wells, have caused great fish kills. So have mine drainage and dozens of other sources from man's technology. The foes of pollution point out that phosphates pumped or dumped into lakes breed jungles of marine plants. The adding of thermally contaminated cooling water from nuclear power plants to the ocean has been described as creating a "thick algal soup" off the shore. It is possible, and much to be desired, that such phenomena be turned to profit rather than loss. Phosphate is a valuable fertilizer and heat is energy, and both might be incorporated into an agriculture or "mariculture" system that will not further wreck the environment but instead contribute to the food basket of the nation.

The Scientific Advisory Committee 1967 Report on the World Food Problem suggests that it may be possible to control the present overfertilization from sewage discharge in estuaries and coastal water and thus produce more fish: "Regulation and control of such nutrients, to the same extent as that required in any deliberate fertilization practice, could potentially transform what is now a public health hazard and a national disgrace into the opportunity for production of valuable marine products."

SAC also suggests using natural hydrodynamic energy or atmospheric energy sources to upwell nutrients for mariculture. Nuclear energy and waste might be used for the same purpose.

Fish Farming

Fish "farming" includes the raising of goldfish and tropical fish, bait, fingerlings for planting streams and lakes, and so on. But there seems much more promise in fish farming for food on a commercial basis. This has been done to a limited extent in ponds in China and Egypt perhaps since several centuries before Christ. Today the Japanese and several other Asian nations practice fish and mollusk culture on a most profitable basis. Trout are raised with a tremendous yield "per acre" for stocking ponds, and some countries use this technique for food fish.

Reservoirs yield fish, and could be made more productive through various techniques. Increased human population means increased needs for water reservoirs. These new reservoirs yield more fish, and if they are fertilized and stocked with feed, output can be further increased. Such enhancement of productivity could cut the need for new inland fisheries. Estimated costs of farm ponds are about $500 an acre.

Freshwater pond cultivation of fish yields from 25 pounds to more than 5 tons an acre, depending on fertility and management. In highly managed, and artificially fed ponds, for instance, up to 16,465 pounds of fish per acre have been produced. In feeding fish meal, grains, and other foods to fish it has been found that trough-fed trout can gain a pound on as little as 1.4 pounds of food. In ponds, with supplemental artificial feeding, catfish gained a pound on 1.5 pounds of food and 0.7 pound of supplemental food produced a gain of a pound in a species called *Tilapia mossambica*.

Trout have also been grown, with supplemental feeding in "raceways" of running water to produce from 5 to 35 tons of fish per acre per year. And carp in Japan have been produced at a phenomenal 500 tons per acre! This figure is misleading to some extent, since much additional feeding is done. However, the yield indicates how small an area is required for the installation— an acre could support about 1,000 people on a diet of fish!

There are about 200 million acres of rice planted a year, and about 30 percent of this area is inundated long enough to grow a crop of fish as well as one of rice. Some Indonesian farmers use this approach, and dual-farm 150,000 acres. In addition to their rice crops they supplement their diet with 45 million pounds of fish, an average of about 300 pounds per acre per year. In those places where supplemental feeding is done, yields can go as high as 1,000 pounds per acre. Even in areas where no attempt is made to farm fish in the paddies, fish sometimes grow in the wild state and it is estimated that around the world about 150,000 tons of such harvest is produced.

The Asian milkfish, or bango, is a classic example. It eats blue-green algae, and is thus an efficient converter of food energy. In Taiwan, Indonesia, and the Philippines, milkfish spawned elsewhere are placed in ponds stocked with the proper algae. Har-

Milkfish being harvested on a fish "farm" at Orani, Bataan, in the
Philippines. Such food production methods meet about 60 percent
of domestic need for protein.
FAO

vesting is easier than "shooting fish in a barrel": the pond is
simply drained and the fish taken. The Rockefeller Foundation is
aiding the Joint Commission on Rural Reconstruction in Taiwan
and the Philippine Fishery Commission in this area. In the latter
country a projected 900,000 acres of mangrove swamps are to be
cleared for pond cultivation of fish.

Unfortunately most farmers either do not feel the need or are
not sold on the idea of combining fish farming with rice farming.
If all the acreage that could produce fish in this way were put
into use, there would be not 45 million pounds of fish added to
tables, but nearly 16 *billion* pounds of fish!

George Borgstrom in his book *The Hungry Planet* describes
Russia's cultivation of carp, with an annual production of 150,000
tons. This exceeds our salmon catch by 50 percent. Borgstrom

reports that the Russians are much interested in fish farming because of weather hazards to agriculture in their country. One
technique combines fish farms with duck ponds; this method permits the ducks to fertilize the plankton fish feed. He also says
that the Russians have successfully accomplished the hybridization of fish and produced several useful new kinds of fish.

T. E. Shelbourne of the Fisheries Laboratory at Lowestoft,
England, suggests pond-raising of plaice and sole. Citing a British
catch of about 35 million plaice a year at considerable expense
and danger, Shelbourne points out that this many fish could be
pond-grown and fed in an area of little more than a square mile.
The British have also successfully grown fish in the warm effluent
from nuclear power plants.

A fish-farming scheme so fantastic as to seem like science fiction
is the brainchild of Japanese fishery scientist Dr. H. Uchihashi.
Using trout, which are traditionally bred in ponds and lakes on an
assembly-line basis and artificially fed, Uchihashi taught the fish
to respond to a bell for feeding, much as Pavlov's dogs were
conditioned. In practice, the trout are slowly accustomed to a
salt-water environment by gradually adding more salt water to
their ponds. During the training period they also are subjected to
a 400-cycle whistle sound for two minutes before pellet feeding
time.

After one month of this Pavlovian conditioning, the trout are
freed to swim at will in the bay. On hearing the dinner bell,
however, they return to the feeding area. Even more interesting,
the fish have learned to tell time, and having been trained to eat
at noon, they start for the "trough" some time before that hour
and are close at hand when the bell rings. The final dinner bell, of
course, is also the harvest signal, unbeknownst to the fattened
trout.

Scots, too, have fertilized the lochs and introduced fish when
plankton growth burgeoned; fish grew as fast in six months as in
two years normally. So we see that pond farming or "aquicul-
ture" may, by degrees, move into the sea for "mariculture."

Aquanaut cowboys, riding herd on schools of fish and aided by trained dolphins and porpoises, may or may not be so much fantasy. Plans for fertilizing the sea itself to increase the growth of either plankton or fish seem doomed, however. To double the nutrient content of the North Sea with artificial fertilizers, for example, would cost fishermen about $40,000 a square mile. The return in fish catch? An estimated $4,000 a square mile, and hardly a paying proposition.

Shellfish Farming

While there has been much success with fish, mollusks offer the best prospects for farming. Some geographers believe that oysters were among man's first food, pointing to the ancient kitchen middens he has heaped with shells. According to Pliny, Romans of his time had progressed to cultivating oysters instead of just gathering the shellfish. Apparently man lost the knack for some time, however. A century ago oyster culture was started in France; its story is finely told in *The Oysters of Locmariaquer* by Eleanor Clark. But the Japanese, with 300 years of experience to back them up, are the oyster champions of the world. Today's most advanced oyster farms are near Hiroshima, in Japan's Inland Sea.

From bamboo rafts floating on barrels, wires hang twenty feet into the water. On the wires are clamshells, and in the summer spawning months billions of oyster larvae attach themselves to the shells. Later the wires are drawn up and cleaned by brushing to remove algae clinging to them. At harvest time a raft thirty by forty-five feet yields two metric tons of oysters, and an acre of marine pasture produces up to 13,000 pounds of oyster flesh a year. To match this yield on land requires the mass-production techniques of a chicken factory—plus a fortune in feed, whereas oysters eat plankton for free. The Japanese also cultivate shrimp on aquatic farms on the island of Shikoku and elsewhere. These retail at from two to four dollars a pound.

America was once the big oyster producer, but as our bays

became polluted Japan took the lead, now producing some 80 million pounds of oyster meat a year. If we could harvest our 10 million potential acres of oyster waters at only the natural rate of 600 pounds per acre per year, the yield would be 6 billion pounds, equal to the total U.S. fish catch. A fifteenfold increase in productivity (the Japanese have increased fiftyfold) would boost this to near the present *total* world fish catch!

Algae Culture

One of the brightest dreams of exploiting the wealth of the sea is the cultivation of algae on a highly efficient basis. A number of researchers, including Arthur D. Little, Inc., in Massachusetts, and others in Japan, have made pilot-plant studies of algae culture as a means of providing food or feed on a much more efficient basis than conventional land farming. While Japan does make some use of this single-celled marine life on a commercial basis, little or no progress has been made elsewhere. As one critic put it, even assuming economical success with production, "you end up with a kind of marine spinach, a greenish powder smelling like moldy hay."

The alga *Chlorella* has been the favorite of the algae culturists for a long time. *Chlorella* cells divide and grow very rapidly. They are high-powered, chlorophyll-loaded photosynthetic champions with no extraneous matter to lower their conversion efficiency. Unlike land plants, algae have no roots, stems, or other nonproductive appendages. In theory, and to some extent in the laboratory runs, phenomenal yields of organic matter are possible. However, the operation as yet has produced none-too-appetizing products at a cost higher than an equivalent amount of fortified flour or fish meal.

Algae culture is not being written off, nevertheless. It is present practice to treat sewage with algae, and the suggestion has been made that the mature scavenger cells be harvested and used as animal feed. Here is a dual process that might be economically attrac-

tive, tapping not only sunlight but also the nutrients in sewage for
fertilizer, an approach somewhat analogous to that of raising fish
in rice paddies.

Despite the failure thus far of algae to provide the food supply
its proponents hope for, some natural forms of algae have long
been used. As seaweed, the stuff sometimes grows to lengths of
300 feet. It is harvested, sometimes by underwater "lawnmowers,"
and used in a variety of ways, from agar for pharmaceutical purposes and as a blender in ice cream production, to direct consumption as food in Japan and some other countries. Algae are
also used as a substrate for the commercial growing of abalone,
a prized and relatively expensive shellfish. At present the best bet
for algae seems as fish food in the pond farming we have been
discussing.

To "Keep" the Catch

As with meat, the problem with fish is keeping it. It spoils
rapidly and noticeably, as Shakespeare often took note in his
plays, commenting on "that ancient and fishlike smell." Fortunately the smoking, drying, or salting of meat works on fish,
too, and historically it has been preserved in this way. In the
fifteenth century William Beukels gave fish lovers the "Dutch
cure" for preserving fish, endowing them with pickled herring.

Freezing has been used for fifty years and more, but it really
didn't come into its own until after World War II. Fish holds in
Gloucester ships were cooled as early as 1840, but to room temperature only. Now the fish are really frozen and kept in that
condition until used. Freezing may take five times as much energy
as the fish possesses as food, however, and this economically rules
out freezing in undeveloped countries.

Fish have also been preserved by irradiation. Unfortunately the
result has been described as "rubbery with a taste of burnt
feathers," or resembling "a dishrag run through a food blender."

Fermenting fish to make a rich and storable sauce was practiced thousands of years ago. The Romans called their fish sauce *garum*, and similar products—called *tuk trey* in Cambodia, *nam pla* in Thailand, and *nuoc nam* in Vietnam—are made today. They have a salty, sharp, cheeselike flavor and substitute nutritionally for milk for babies, being high in protein and rich in amino acids. Indochina alone consumes 10 million gallons of the stuff a year.

One man's fish sauce is another man's poison, however, and other ways of converting fish have been developed. An example is fish "sausage," made from a variety of fish, including the buffalo fish grown in rice fields of some of our southern states. Fish "ham rolls" are another example of attempts to camouflage seafood.

Fish Protein Concentrate

In 1964 the world sea catch contained 17.1 billion pounds of protein, enough for 10 grams a day for 2 billion people. This amount didn't get to all of them, unfortunately. The most skillful camouflage doesn't seem to sell all the fish men can harvest, no matter how much the reluctant customer needs protein. At times the catch can't even be given away, so more drastic measures must be taken.

Not all of us are fish lovers, and not all fish lovers are wild about all fish. But English epigrammatist John Heywood once remarked "All is fish that cometh to net," and so, by definition at least, any fish is fair game. Here is one epigram that works, and all fish can be processed successfully into fish protein concentrate, or FPC. FPC has a protein content of 80 percent by weight, and a yield of 15 percent of the original weight. If an average person needs twenty grams of animal protein a day, a harvest of 200 million tons of fish converted to FPC would supply the protein needs of the world population. A 2-billion-ton catch, thought possible by some, would furnish sufficient protein for 33 billion humans! The low estimate of fish harvest is three times the present catch; the high one is thirty times as great.

Technician grinding whole fish as first step in preparing highly nutritious, protein-rich fish flour. This work is being done at the Bureau of Commercial Fisheries laboratories at Beltsville, Maryland.
Bureau of Commercial Fisheries

Sold on the idea of converting fish into a wholesome and rich meal or flour for use as a supplement in cooking, a number of research laboratories got busy learning how to convert whole fish, from small shellfish to whales—"all that cometh to net," and then some—into fish protein concentrate. They succeeded, producing a powder containing practically all protein and no odor. Ironically, the first snag they hit wasn't consumer rejection; it came instead from a guardian of the consumer.

The U.S. Food and Drug Administration banned the consumption of whole fish flour, saying it was considered "filthy," since bones, scales, eyes, and even guts were used. A senator objected, saying that FDA had already approved the sale of "grasshoppers which are not filleted" and "chocolate-covered ants on which *no* preliminary cleaning work was done." The FDA finally relented and accepted the FPC process used by the Bureau of Commercial Fisheries at Beltsville, Maryland, for converting whole hake into a yellowish-white powder.

The victory was a hollow one, as it turned out. If you have baked bread or made gravy with FPC you are in a distinct minority. Some people like fish sauce; some can stand ersatz sausage and ham because they enjoyed the original meat. But FPC was like nothing ever seen or tasted before. Maybe it was just like nothing. At any rate, sales have not been heavy, and any fears of turning all the fish catch into FPC at the expense of tuna fillets, salmon steaks, or whale blubber were soon dispelled. Only about 20 percent of the catch is being turned into anything besides fish, and most of that portion produces, not FPC for humans, but conventional fish meal destined to become chicken and hog feed.

The idea of using fish for purposes other than direct human nourishment is perhaps only a little newer than the idea of fishing itself. The Pilgrims learned from the Algonquin Indians to put gizzard shad or menhaden into the same hole with a few grains of corn at planting time to produce better crops. Several hundred years earlier Marco Polo had reported the feeding of fish to cows, sheep, camels, and horses in early China; by the nineteenth century fish-eating cows were a commonplace in New England.

Each year some 26 billion pounds of fish goes through the grinder and comes out as 4 billion pounds of meal. This is between 60 and 70 percent animal protein, with all the essential amino acids. It has more phosphorus and calcium than do plants, and mixed with alfalfa and bran it makes a feed that animals do not turn up their noses at. It is a tribute to nature's chemistry that your chicken (fed almost 60 percent on fish meal) doesn't taste of the sea!

Some nutritionists rage because so much of the sea's harvest is not eaten by man but by livestock and chickens. But part of the problem is that some starving peoples literally turn up their noses at food they are not used to or not attracted to. We can get them to eat candy bars and Eskimo Pies and drink Coca-Cola, but fortified fish meal and protein-packed algae are something else again.

Still hopeful, the FPC people at the Bureau of Commercial

Fisheries have worked up cost estimates calling for six fifteen-ton-a-day processing plants and two specially built 120-foot catching and processing ships. Altogether these would come to about $5.5 million, and would provide one "mega-ration" of FPC, the amount sufficient to give one billion people their needed animal proteins daily. The cost would be a modest 13.9 cents per pound for almost pure protein.

Whether the green granaries of the sea will be man's salvation remains to be seen. Surely they represent a great reserve of excellent protein source, and developments such as Peru's emergence as a major fishing nation are encouraging. Despite Huxley's optimism, man might well exhaust the bounty of the sea if he set his mind to fully exploiting it. However, he is a long way from that point today. God promised us dominion over the sea—the rest is up to us.

Part III.

Solving the Problems

Whoever could make two ears of corn, or two blades of
grass to grow where only one grew before, would
deserve better of mankind and do more essential service
to his country, than the whole race of politicians put
together.

Jonathan Swift, *Gulliver's Travels*

CHAPTER 10

The Green Revolution

How do you feed 2 percent more people each year? In the
United States there is no problem; we continue to cut back
acreage and still increase our yield of crops. Here are examples
of such improvement (100 kilograms per hectare are roughly
equivalent to 90 pounds per acre):

	CORN	SOYBEANS	WHEAT
1951–55	2,600	1,345	1,120 (Kg. per hectare)
1961–65	4,426	1,628	1,690 (Kg. per hectare)

The corn crop of 1969, about 4.3 billion bushels, was the third
largest in this country's history, although it was grown on the
smallest acreage used since records have been kept! Yet D. E.
Alexander, a leading corn-breeding expert at the University of
Illinois, is quoted as speaking emphatically of "quantum jumps"
still ahead in corn development, even compared to the miracles
already accomplished with hybridization.

In 1969, in the face of 14 percent fewer acres of wheat planted
in the United States, the drop in production was less than 10
percent, showing an increase of about 4 percent in productivity.

1968 harvests of miracle wheat in India were so abundant that storage
for the grain was lacking in many localities. Here is surplus piled in
the street of a village.
The Rockefeller Foundation

The average yield was about thirty bushels per acre, and that will
climb as more acreage is planted to the new dwarf strains that are
more productive; Gaines, for example, and a newer one called
Blueboy. The wheat carry-over or surplus was up 50 percent
from the previous year. Farmers now say it is foolish to consider
grain as food with such surpluses and such low prices; they look
on it only as feed. Soybeans have produced up to a hundred
bushels an acre. Here also is a question of what value the crop will
be except as feed, since it, too, will be available in great surplus
quantities.

   It is ironic to say that, despite some hunger and malnutrition
in the United States, our bigger worry is how to keep from get-

ting fat rather than starving. Nor are we alone in being well fed. Much of Europe, with a slow population growth, is in a good food position. Japan is managing well. Canada exports grain, as do Argentina and Australia. Mexico is moving toward self-sufficiency and even a position as an exporter. The problem areas are Asia, Africa, and parts of South America, all with high rates of population growth and a poor record of food production.

In developing lands the food problem is even worse than the population increase of 2 percent a year would indicate. Those people already on hand are not getting a proper shake at the dinner table, and to catch up it is necessary, or at least desirable, to jump food production by *more* than 2 percent each year. India is presently doing that, increasing her output by about 4 percent in the face of a rising population amounting to about 2.5 percent a year. That's a net bonus of 1.5 percent for better diets for everyone, or at least those to whom the extra food is distributed.

Asia has enjoyed several good years of agricultural crops, after some very bad years in 1965 and 1966. Should there be a recurrence of the bad years, the picture could quickly change from green plenty to black famine. And U.S. and other surpluses would change as quickly to deficits. The developing nations cannot feed the world, now or in the foreseeable future. So the developing nations must become self-sufficient, and remain so.

The Rockefeller Foundation laid it on the line in the "President's Review," 1966:

. . . While debating the moral obligation of the developed nations of the world, most especially the United States, to provide food for the hungry, we have seen supplies of so-called surpluses dwindle alarmingly. The net effect has been a practical example of the inability of a relatively small sector of the world to feed, on any continuing basis, significantly large sectors. Any attempt to sustain such an effort over a period of years will not only fail in its objective but will also substantially impair the economies of the donor nations. There is only one alternative: to bring more of the underproducing countries, whose agrarian proficiency at present is only minimal, to the point where they can produce food for their own needs or other commodities which can be exchanged for food.

This alternative, which is not only highly desirable but absolutely necessary, postulates three major requirements:

1. A clear-cut understanding on the part of national leaders everywhere that agriculture is an industry and must be treated as such, with the same intelligence and support which is applied to any other industry;

2. Broad improvements in conventional agriculture through (a) applying to existing crop acreage those conversion factors which have been demonstrated to lead from underproduction to full production, (b) the increasing utilization of the humid tropics for growing food and feed, and (c) the greater utilization of lands not now in production because of their aridity;

3. Vastly increased research on nonconventional sources of food and on the protein enrichment of those basic food cereals which are the staple nourishment of most of the world's peoples.

Faced with the need to produce more food, a farmer has two obvious choices: He can farm more land, as American farmers did during World War II, or he can produce more on the land he is already cultivating. Ideally the two methods should be combined. Since the second approach demands a higher level of technology than some developing countries now possess, let us first consider the seemingly simpler choice of breaking new ground that can be farmed by existing methods and yield additional food for the growing population.

The "New Lands" Approach

In 1951 C. E. Kellogg of the U.S. Department of Agriculture estimated 4.5 billion acres of arable land in the world, but by 1964 had upped the figure to 6.6 billion acres. Economist Colin Clark uses a more sophisticated method of calculating total arable land. Calling one-crop acreage "standard land," he applies proportionate fractions or multiples to land that is less or more productive than standard land. For instance, he rates the tropics at from two to five times the productivity of standard one-crop

land, if sufficient fertilizer can be used along with proper farming techniques. These conversion factors lead to an estimate of 19
to 26.4 billion *equivalent* arable acres.

The Scientific Advisory Committee arrives at a much more
conservative estimate of 7.9 billion acres of potential arable land,
of which about 850 million acres would require irrigation to
produce even one crop. Nevertheless, SAC says the area of potentially arable land on the Earth is much larger than previously
supposed, being about 24 percent of the total ice-free land surface
and considerably more than twice the area that has been cultivated during the last few decades. It is more than three times the
area actually harvested in any given year.

There is little potential arable land in the Soviet Union, Europe,
or Asia. It is true that Israel is turning desert into farmland, and
even experimenting with crops that grow in salt water, to provide
more food for that fledgling nation. In the first decade following
World War II the net harvest acreage in Asia increased by about
2 percent a year, but since 1957 this has declined to about 1.1
percent a year, and even this slight increase cannot continue.
Perhaps an additional 200 million acres could be irrigated, but this
would cost an estimated $80 billion.

More than half the potentially arable land in the world, over
4 billion acres, is in the tropics; 30 percent in humid lands, 36
percent in the subhumid, and the remaining 34 percent in the arid
or semiarid regions. The bulk of this, some 3 billion acres, lies in
Africa and South America, which except for Europe and Australia have the smallest cultivated areas in the world. Accordingly,
many food experts are optimistic for South America and Africa.
According to SAC, the limiting factors in those countries will not
be natural resources but economic, institutional, and social problems. Admittedly many tropic soils are low in fertility, they point
out, but so was Florida soil, which is now productive.

Australia has demonstrated that it can produce cattle on a
booming scale on land that once supported only kangaroos and
wild dogs. It has been so successful it is a big exporter. Even on

the native spear grass, Aussie ranchers ran cattle that in six years produced stringy beef at least suitable for hamburger, and some profit. Recently a plant called "Townsend lucerne" (lucerne is England's word for what we call alfalfa) was accidentally introduced, perhaps from a Brazilian ship. It grows like a weed, is high in protein, and with fertilizer is expected to increase beef production sixfold. This is in the tropics, with its typical high energy yield of sunlight, and areas of more than twenty inches of rain a year. Even without full availability of the new lucerne for its cattle, Australia has already more than doubled the cattle production of all of Texas. Australia now produces beef at ten cents a pound cheaper than that raised in the United States. With development it is expected that Australian ranchers can further cut their costs and one day raise ten times as much livestock as they now do.

Opinions are not unanimous on the "new lands" approach, however. As long ago as 1945 Frank Pearson and Floyd Harper, writing in *The World's Hunger,* pointed out that there were large areas of leached-out soils in the tropics, eliminating such areas from commercial agriculture "as effectively as inadequate rainfall eliminated the Sahara Desert." Today the Paddocks belittle the "equatorial wonderlands in the heart of the Amazon Basin," pointing out that in less than five years one such project turned lateritic soil into "virtual pavements of rock."

"If Brazil has so much land waiting for the plow," Paul and William Paddock, authors of *Famine—1975,* demand, "why do the farmers of its starving Northeast continue to lead such wretched lives on their hopeless soils?" They are equally scathing about the prospects of double-cropping in tropical lands, pointing out the failure of one such project they managed. In their opinion, only 7 percent—not 24 percent—of the Earth's land mass combines proper soil texture, nutrients, temperature, topography, and precipitation to permit what they call normal agriculture.

Certainly the development taking place in Australia shows that we can add to the food basket of the world. But it is easy to oversimplify to the point of distorting out of all reason the new lands idea. It takes money to clear those lands, to irrigate them, and to cultivate them. Land costs money to buy, and more money for maintenance and taxes. And money is the key problem of underdeveloped peoples. If they had money they could *buy* more food. Another problem is the time lag; one doesn't farm new land overnight. Still another problem is that there is perhaps good reason for land never having been farmed before. Poor soil is an example; poor drainage or shortage of water are others.

In our own country there have been some incredible blunders with the new lands approach. A small fortune was spent in developing water for an area in Wyoming called Cottonwood Bench. After the irrigation system was in, it was learned that the land being watered was such bad soil that nobody could make a living on it anyway! How such a monumental goof could occur is a mystery, but it did—and in our highly developed country and administered by government scientists and technicians. What then could happen in an underdeveloped land, short of scientists and technicians knowledgeable in land and crops?

The day may come, although it is not inevitable, when even marginal lands must be put into good enough condition to produce food. That day is not yet here, for most experts agree that there can be great improvements in crop yields of existing farmland—enough improvement to take care of twice as many people, and more if necessary.

More Food Per Acre

In its 1967 report to the President, the Scientific Advisory Committee concentrated on the concept of increased yields on existing lands:

Production of major food crops can be increased substantially in both developed and developing countries. Application of existing knowledge in the form of coordinated, crop-oriented research and production programs will be needed—especially in the food-deficit

Nobel Prize winner Dr. Norman E. Borlaug is shown recording the vigor and stage of growth of wheat in a breeding plot. *USDA*

nations—if food requirements of the 1970s and 1980s are to be satisfied. Even under the most favorable circumstances, the interval between inauguration of such programs and their realization will be at least 5 to 10 years.

Existing food deficits, and the possibility that these may further increase within the foreseeable future, emphasize the critical need for intensification of plant production. That plant production can be intensified appears to be obvious from a comparison of yields between developed and developing countries, of current yields with those of a few decades ago, and of the rates at which yields are increasing in some countries. For example, yields of basic food crops, such as the cereal grains and potatoes, are from 50 to 350 percent higher in many of the developed countries than in most of the developing ones. During the past decade and a half, increases in yields differ by the same general order of magnitude. Even in the most agriculturally advanced countries, average yields are much less than the theoretical limits based on absorption and utilization of solar radiation.

The following table documents the great differences in productivity from country to country for various crops. It is interesting

to compare Japanese yields with those of the United States (100
kilograms per hectare roughly equals 90 pounds per acre).

1964–65 Comparative Yields
(*Kilograms per Hectare*)

	BRAZIL	INDIA	JAPAN	PAKISTAN	U.S.
Maize	1,160	990	2,330	1,080	3,930
Sorghums and millet	—	990	2,560	990	2,580
Potatoes	6,000	8,300	17,800	7,700	20,700
Sweet potatoes and yams	10,100	6,400	19,800	—	9,400
Dry beans	620	280	770	530	1,360
Dry peas	—	520	1,000	—	1,730
Dry broad beans	370	—	1,060	—	—
Soybeans	850	—	1,110	—	1,530
Peanuts	1,440	870	2,070	980	1,760

SOURCE: Table adapted from Scientific Advisory Committee, 1967 Report on the World Food Problem.

The next table shows yield increases over a fifteen-year period
and indicates problem areas in the agricultural world. The disappointing performances of Brazil, India, and Pakistan do not,

Increasing Yields of
Rice and Wheat Worldwide
(*Kilograms per Hectare*)

	1948–53	1962–63	1963–64	1964–65
		RICE		
Brazil	1,570	1,540	1,520	—
India	1,110	1,370	1,550	1,610
Japan	4,250	5,280	5,230	5,150
Pakistan	1,380	1,510	1,720	1,680
United States	2,560	4,180	4,440	4,590
		WHEAT		
Brazil	740	950	490	880
India	660	890	790	730
Japan	1,850	2,540	1,230	2,450
Pakistan	870	820	830	830
United States	1,120	1,690	1,700	1,770

SOURCE: Table adapted from Scientific Advisory Committee, 1967 Report on the World Food Problem.

however, reflect the recent and encouraging improvements made with the new hybrid crops.

Fertilization, mechanization, hybridization, and pest control have increased yields in the United States and other countries to the point that more than 200 bushels of wheat have been produced on a single acre, and comparable yields of corn are demonstrated. Average yields, although not up to these contest-winning feats, are remarkable in that they are several times those customary in underdeveloped countries. And the green-thumb idea is beginning to spread.

The Seeds of Revolution

In its 1967 report the Scientific Advisory Committee listed a program for helping the developing nations feed themselves:

1. Attention to basic food crops that can be propagated rapidly— wheat, rice, maize, pulses, oil-seed legumes, sorghum, millet, potato, sweet potato, yams, cassava, and banana. Attempts toward self-sufficiency in specialized, poorly adapted crops should be avoided.
2. Substantial breeding efforts, in the regions and by the nations where the crops are to be used, should be encouraged.
3. Establishment of organizations that can produce and supply adequate and dependable quantities of high-quality seed. Generally, private enterprise has been much more effective than government monopolies in producing and distributing seeds of improved varieties and hybrids.
4. Establishment of integrated national crop-oriented programs under unified leadership.
5. Plant breeders must utilize high levels of soil fertility in breeding programs in order to develop plant types capable of converting large amounts of nutrients into end products of better nutritional quality.

All this must have rung familiarly in the ears of those who had been working for more than twenty years in some of the developing lands. For what the committee suggested was no more than an extension of efforts that underlay the green revolution that

Former U.S. Secretary of Agriculture Orville Freeman examines vegetables with Vietnam's Minister of Agriculture, Lam Van Tri. Demonstrations proved the value of fertilizers and pesticides.
USDA

blossomed late in the 1960s. The seeds of that revolution had been planted by dedicated scientists and field men long years before.

Among those involved were the U.N.'s Food and Agriculture Organization, the U.S. Agency for International Development, foreign government agencies, and a number of private organizations—among which the Ford Foundation, W. K. Kellogg Foundation, and Rockefeller Foundation rank high in their efforts. Two decades of work in Mexico led to such developments as the International Maize and Wheat Improvement Center in Mexico, the International Rice Research Institute in the Philippines, centers for tropical agriculture research in Nigeria and Colombia, and the Inter-Asian Corn Improvement Program in Thailand.

At the time of India's independence in 1947 she was using less fertilizer on her 320 million acres than Belgium on 2.5 million. India had, and still has, far more cattle than she can properly feed. Asked for assistance, in 1950 the Ford Foundation drew up a "package of practices" for India, pointing out what must be done: credit for farmer, fertilizer, pesticides, improved seeds and implements, price supports, and technical assistance.

The agricultural aid programs bore some fruit. From 1950 to 1960, in the face of a population increase from 363 million to 450 million, food consumption in India was increased per capita from 13.8 ounces to about 16 ounces of grain per day. Ford continued to assist, and by 1966 had spent nearly $12 million in Indian assistance programs. Adoption of Japanese-type rice mills resulted in fewer broken kernels, and experts from Louisiana State University showed the Indians how to reduce milling losses from 40 percent to 34 percent and less, providing an additional 5 million tons of grain for the country annually.

One-fourth of the world's grain harvest is wheat. In ten years this increased from 171 to 250 million tons. Corn production worldwide increased in the same ten years from 138 million tons to 220 million tons, gaining on wheat. Total world food production rose from about 600 million tons in 1946 to 1,088 million tons in 1966. The agricultural miracle in the making seemed to have arrived.

Miracles are seldom worked overnight, however. Despite the excellent work, worldwide results were hidden—largely by the shadow of bad weather in Asia in 1965 and 1966. Soon America was shipping 10 million tons of grain to India on a crash basis to avert starvation for millions of that country's people, and appreciable quantities were sent to Pakistan as well. The situation was hailed as the "world food crisis" and many U.S. farmers responded by planting and harvesting bumper crops of wheat and other grains to fight starvation in underdeveloped lands. Several ships a day, carrying thousands of tons of wheat, left our ports. As many as thirty at a time were tied up at docks in Bombay waiting as much as a month to unload—while hungry natives also waited in the streets for relief workers to weigh out their rations on small scales. But the picture of famine and a long, bleak outlook for India changed quickly. And that is the change that is known as the "green revolution."

The revolution in farming began for the underdeveloped countries in Mexico, long an importer of grains. With help mainly from the Ford and Rockefeller foundations, that country began slowly to exploit new plant species. A new dwarf strain of wheat from Japan, which pioneered in the discovery of dwarfing factors —aided by the fortunate find of a single natural hybrid plant in an African wheat field!—was the basis for the new Mexican revolution. The Japanese dwarf, the Norin strain, was brought to the United States, too, and developed into Gaines wheat, which has produced up to 216 bushels per acre.

Over a period of years average Mexican wheat yields increased from about eleven to more than forty bushels per acre. Corn yields more than doubled. Potato yields tripled. Finally, with the dwarf wheat strain, Mexico no longer had to buy wheat to feed her people; she even began exporting it to feed the hungry in other lands. And in 1968 the Rockefeller Foundation could report:

By 1963 it had been clearly demonstrated in Mexico, that, with organized assistance, a food-deficit nation could rapidly modernize its agriculture. . . . Yet the Rockefeller Foundation was still the only major organization with career staff engaged, on an international scale, directly in applied research on the basic food crops. . . . Today unprecedented production increases are being achieved in some areas of food-deficit nations. New terms have been coined—"miracle rice," "the green revolution"—in attempts to characterize these exciting new developments. . . . It is in fact difficult to list all the regions now benefiting, for example, from the use of the wheats from Mexico, so rapidly and so widely are they being adopted.

There have now been enough successes to demonstrate clearly that most nations can, if they will, dramatically and rapidly increase agricultural output. . . .

In mid-1965, Pakistan bought 350 tons of dwarf seed wheat from Mexico. India was also one of Mexico's customers. Faced with serious food shortages after two years of bad weather and poor crops, the Indian government in 1966 bought a huge amount of dwarf seed wheat—18,000 tons of it, the biggest such purchase up to that time. Yields went up remarkably, aided partly by good weather for the next two years—and India had so much wheat that the stuff piled up in the streets for a better place to store it!

Yields that had traditionally been about 11 or 12 bushels an acre were now up to 60 and 70 bushels, and one grower in Punjabi won a prize for producing 150 bushels of spring wheat on a single acre. And India had wheat to sell for anybody who wanted to buy. Meanwhile, back in the United States, farmers found themselves left with bumper surpluses of wheat, for which they were lucky to get a dollar a bushel as animal feed. Spurred by the success of her dwarf wheat imports, India set a goal of doubling wheat production in eight years. She also jumped sorghum output per acre as much as twenty times what was produced not long before. Millet was coaxed to grow in ninety days or less, and to produce three crops a year.

In 1967 Turkey set a new record for seed wheat purchases, ordering 22,000 tons from Mexico, and Pakistan soon upped the ante to a whopping 42,000 tons. Yields began to soar in these countries, too.

Thailand added corn to its crops (historically mostly rice) and, with a new flint variety imported from Guatemala, soon produced enough for her own needs and for export, principally to Japan in successful competition with United States corn.

In the Philippines, a miracle rice called IR8, introduced in Taiwan and developed by the International Rice Research Institute, was put into production and is doubling yields per acre. IR8 is a short-strawed rice that can use up to 120 pounds of fertilizer an acre, compared with the average of 35 pounds that local varieties could tolerate. Four years after the Philippines got IR8

Turkish Minister of Agriculture, Bahri Dagdas, (left) celebrates with villagers the success of new wheat imported from Mexico.
The Rockefeller Foundation

they were self-sufficient in rice for the first time since 1905. Despite a nine-month drought, the worst in a century, the 1969 crop was sufficient, helping President Marcos to be reelected to his office, the first president so honored in Philippines history.

The miracle rice has been introduced in Asia and India and does as well there. Now there is a "super-miracle" strain that does 15 percent better than IR8. Other developments are early-maturing rice (120 days instead of 150 to 200), and control of the stem borer (an insect that attacks rice plants) by putting lindane pellets in the irrigation water. This method works much better than spraying with insecticide.

In addition to hybrids in corn, wheat, and rice, hybrid barley has been developed. Robert T. Ramage, Professor of Agronomy

at the University of Arizona has worked out a method he calls
BTT, for "balanced tertiary trisomic," which produces barley
populations that are genetically male sterile. These then serve as
the female parents of hybrid barley. Ramage's hybrids are being
grown in the field, and he is now breeding a dwarf plant into the
line to prevent the lodging that results with the extra burden of
heavier production. Ramage has also developed new methods of
planting and water management that also increase yield of grains.
Interestingly, he found that while management could increase
yields by about 25 percent and the hybrid strains could add as
much, the combination of both in the same planting produced
increases of as much as 60 percent.

Ramage used irradiation techniques with his hybrids; other
barley geneticists have experimented with DDT spray to achieve
sterile plants. Genetic male sterility techniques are also used with
castor beans and spinach.

An increase of only 4 percent in crop yield in India seems to belie
the extravagant claims of doubled production. Thus far, however,
only a fraction of Asia's lands have been planted to the new
miracle grains. And fertilization and mechanization do not yet
match those of developed farming lands like North America and
Western Europe.

Another factor puts the frosting on the cake. In the United
States high yields are produced despite our being in the temperate
zone, where the sun's energy is moderate. The food problem areas
of the world are largely in the tropics, where there is generally
more sun and more rain. In theory, and in some tests, yields in
Asia and elsewhere in tropical climates have gone far beyond the
best achieved in America.

More Miracles

There is yet another way to increase the amount of food
available to a hungry world, beyond producing more of it per
acre or planting more acres. That is to improve the food itself.

Some dramatic strides have been made in this direction, and more are surely in the offing.

Corn is a most important crop in much of the world; it feeds many humans and even more animals. But corn is low in two vital amino acids in its protein department, lysine and tryptophane. Just a few years ago, however, scientists succeeded in genetically adding more lysine to corn. Results are encouraging, and it is probable that corn will soon be providing much more of the protein needs of those who eat it.

In 1963 two Purdue scientists discovered that a mutant gene called "opaque-2" was directly related to the level of the amino acid lysine in corn. Breeding a corn line with opaque-2 produced grain containing ten times the normal amount of lysine, and also more tryptophane, another vital amino acid. This was no laboratory curiosity, as feeding tests with rats and then swine proved. The new high-lysine corn had nearly the value of casein, a milk protein used as a reference standard in nutrition. Further study turned up another corn variant called "floury-2," with even more lysine than opaque-2. At first the high lysines had low yield per acre, but strains were soon developed that yielded within 95 percent of that of normal corn.

At Chapingo, Mexico, a Rockefeller-funded laboratory gives plant geneticists access to nearly 10,000 varieties of wheat and corn, a collection painstakingly built up over nearly thirty years of work. India's Agricultural Research Institute at New Delhi does similar work with sorghum and the millets, with some 7,800 sorghum strains to work with. And the International Rice Research Institute in Los Baños, in the Philippines, does protein studies, selecting from among 10,000 strains of rice to come up with higher protein crops of this cereal. Unlike corn, rice has amino acids of the right kind—until we polish it—but it is very low in total protein. While there has been no dramatic breakthrough, as with high-lysine corn, work goes on to increase the protein content of rice. Some researchers are also trying to find strains of rice that will flower and set seed in long-daylight climates.

Students at the International Rice Research Institute in the Philippines
weed an experimental plot of miracle rice.
The Rockefeller Foundation

Horn of Plenty

As late as 1967 Lester Brown, administrator of the U.S. Department of Agriculture's Foreign Agriculture Service, was warning:

This flood of people is washing away the benefits of millions of man-
years of effort and billions of dollars in foreign aid. . . . Only five
years ago the United Nations coined the years 1960 to 1970 the Decade
of Development. If the adverse food/population trends of the first
half of this decade are not reversed, it may well be recorded as the
Decade of Disappointment.

By mid-1968 Brown could speak confidently of the agricultural

revolution in the Asian countryside stretching from Turkey to
the Philippines, and including the pivotal countries of India and
Pakistan. He had the facts to document his encouragement. India's
total food grain crop was estimated at 100 million tons, up 32
percent over the drought of the preceding year, and 12 percent
higher than the previous high. Pakistan had a wheat crop 30 percent above its previous record, and Ceylon's rice harvest had
climbed 13 percent above the old record crop. Iran had become a
wheat exporter.

Farmers were finding it profitable to use fertilizers and other
technological inputs, often for the first time in Asian agriculture.
Pesticides, too, were paying off, now that rice was averaging
from 3,000 to 4,000 pounds per acre instead of the customary
1,000 to 1,500 pounds. In the Punjabi region, Pakistani farmers put
down 32,000 private "tube wells," at costs from $1,000 to $2,500
apiece—and generally were able to pay for them in two years.
Thai farmers were hiring their plowing done by tractor, rather
than feeding water buffalo all year to have draft power available.

Brown pointed out that AID had trained some 4,000 Asian
agriculturists during the last decade, and that it was helping build
fertilizer plants in India, Taiwan, Iran, Malaysia, the Philippines,
and South Korea. These he expected to boost food-producing
capacity by 25 million tons a year. And new rice strains promised
double- or even triple-cropping, or the planting of rice in combination with grain sorghum and corn.

Brown also touched on another very important result of the
green revolution in *Foreign Affairs*, Volume 46:

> The positive economic effects of an agricultural takeoff in Asian
> countries are quite evident. What is not so readily realized is that it
> will bolster the confidence of national leaders in their ability to handle
> other seemingly insoluble problems. It may also strengthen their faith
> in modern technology and its potential for improving the well-being
> of their people.

The Rockefeller Foundation Annual Report for 1968 agreed:

Perhaps the most profound change that has taken place in India during the past five years has been the altered attitude of national and local leaders and the consequent redirection of scientific efforts toward production problems. Apathy is giving way to excitement regarding present and potential agricultural progress; hope has replaced the sense of helplessness that once prevailed. Agriculture is increasingly being recognized as an industry of fundamental importance to the economic development of the nation.

Concrete proof of this recognition lies in the fact that India has increased the number of universities specializing in agricultural science by ten, and in a single year graduated 7,300 bachelor of science degrees and 804 advanced degrees.

All a Mirage?

For some of those concerned with the food problem, the sudden switch from famine to food on hand was a fluke. There was even a hint of displeasure tinging some of the criticism—disappointment or incredulity that the situation was better. Some writers sarcastically commented on "miracle rats" bred on the new miracle grains. The *Population Bulletin* of December 1968 derided the green revolution under the headline "Mr. Brown Turns Green":

Recent months have produced an astonishing reversal of official attitudes toward the food-population situation. Caught up in the euphoria of a proclaimed "Green Revolution," some U.S. Government spokesmen see worldwide food surpluses just around the corner. The U.S. Department of Agriculture has flip-flopped on this question with notable agility. In a review of the world food situation released in August 1967—just 17 months after Secretary Freeman's earlier warnings [of a forthcoming food crisis]—the Department announced: "The combined excess food production capacity of all the developed countries in 1980 will be more than adequate to provide for the increased food import needs of the less developed countries. This is likely even if the less developed countries do not improve their rate of growth in grain production."

Proud Indian farmer displays prize millet, another result of "green revolution" research.
The Rockefeller Foundation

This new-found knack of looking at the future through a green-tinted crystal ball is perhaps best exemplified by Lester Brown, Administrator of the Department of Agriculture's Foreign Agricultural Service. As recently as 1967, he shared the cautious pessimism of most of his colleagues. Speaking at Kansas University in December 1968, however, he suggested that the population crisis might have to be renamed:

"Thus far, during the 1960s the population problem has always been equated with the food-population problem. This may not always be so. By 1980 the population problem will more likely be referred to as the employment-population problem."

Neither were the Paddocks pleased with the green revolution, as they indicated in an interview in 1969 in the *Rotarian:*

We have not seen this popularly-called "miracle-rice" in production in Asia, but we have seen it in Latin America. There, it has not been successful either agronomically or commercially. Even in Asia the new rice is not as well liked by most consumers as are the old standard varieties, and it generally commands a lower price in the market place.

We are particularly worried about all the farmers in a region suddenly switching to a new variety of rice because we fear that some unknown insect or fungus may be lying in wait for it. With everybody growing the same variety of rice which has been superficially tested, an epiphytotic disease [a plant disease that tends to recur sporadically and to affect large numbers of plants] could break out with disastrous results. Most agronomists are aware of this and fear the latent danger.

The International Maize and Wheat Improvement Center in Mexico is an excellent concept. However, during an extensive research trip in Mexico and Central America this year our personal observation is that after 30 years of work on corn hybrids by the Rockefeller Foundation the resulting corns remain an unimportant part of the foundation of the *small* farmers. Some Rockefeller Foundation figures we have seen say that 17 percent of Mexico's corn land is planted to its improved varieties. Perhaps this is true, but we certainly were unable to verify any such high figure by talking with Mexican farmers. Even if the figure were true, it serves to illustrate how difficult it is to institute a radical change in a nation's agriculture.

Of the miracle wheat, the Paddocks said it was truly a great strain, but that subsidies and government price supports should get equal credit for increased production. They were highly critical of the feasibility of transferring fertilizer technology, since rice farmers in India pay three or four times as much for fertilizer relatively as do the Japanese, and those in Thailand pay more than five times as much.

Referring to FAO claims of 9,500 field trials of fertilizer showing overall average yield increases of 74 percent, with produce twice the cost of fertilizer, Dr. Forrest Hill, a former vice-president of Ford Foundation, said he had seen farmers who couldn't write or read but never one who couldn't figure. Hill wondered why farmers weren't agitating for fertilizer.

It has also been pointed out that when new irrigation systems

were put in, the dreaded parasitic disease schistosomiasis sometimes struck down the people in the area. Spread by a water snail,
which takes advantage of the new waterways, and nearly impossible to check, the disease forced the shutting down of one new
land development in Rhodesia and caused havoc in many other
locations.

Visible Means of Support

Despite its critics, however, most of the evidence seemed to
indicate that Mr. Brown's green revolution was no mirage. In an
on-the-scene report a newsman returning to India after an absence
of seventeen years wrote in *U.S. News and World Report* for
May 25, 1970:

Progress is at long last visible in a country that has swallowed up
9 billion dollars of U.S. aid and some billions more from Soviet
Russia. . . .
    At the same time, a "green revolution" is taking hold. Food supply
is growing 5 percent annually, twice as fast as population. More grain
is produced, less is wasted. With no more than average luck in
weather, India could be feeding itself by 1972. . . .
    Many highways, once choked with countless bullock carts mo-
nopolizing the middle, now have almost as many tractors as carts.
More cars and trucks whiz along the road center with shrieking horns.

Described in detail was the village of Berkhurd in the Ludhiana
district of Punjab State, "where 700 people live quite differently
than in 1953." A link will soon connect it with the Grand Trunk
Road. There are more brick houses than mud now, and more than
fifty drilled wells, even though these cost about 3,000 rupees
(about $400) each. Farmers are also beginning to order Indian-
built "Escort" tractors to replace bullocks, oxen, and camels.
Dung is being used for fertilizer instead of fuel, and a fine of 100
rupees is levied on those who do use it for cooking.

Robert McNamara, head of the World Bank, told an audience
at Notre Dame in 1969:

Wholesale famine is not inevitable. . . . We have been given time to avert the situation by those who have created the revolution in agricultural technology. . . . It is a revolution which has expanded the number of acres sown with the new seeds from 200 in 1965 to 20 million in 1968 and an estimated 34 million in 1969. If we will but speed the spread of this agricultural revolution—by adequate and properly administered technical and financial assistance to the developing countries—we can expect that for the next two decades the world's food supply will grow at a faster rate than its population.

Lane Palmer, editor of *Farm Journal,* was even more optimistic in a speech to the American Institute of Cooperation, August 1969:

> Granted there are still many hungry people. But their hunger results more from decrepit economic and political systems, from poorer distribution methods and from a dearth of education rather than from a dearth of available food.

Palmer makes this prognosis of the food situation ahead:

> . . . the picture I paint is not of a world food crisis, but the problem of plenty:
> *In the developing countries,* a dramatic increase in irrigation, the building of fertilizer plants, the breeding of improved cereal varieties, and a transition from being grain importers to becoming grain exporters until such time as their economies can stimulate and support an animal agriculture.
> *In the maturing economies* of Argentina, Australia, New Zealand, Canada, Mexico and Western Europe, a continuing push for agricultural self-sufficiency, increasing competition with the U.S. for the world grain markets, and increasing export of animal products to other developed countries, including the U.S. itself.
> *And in the United States,* continuing acceleration of productivity per acre and per animal, continuing large profit margins for the farmers and corporations who are first in adopting the new technology, heavy price pressures on producers who are reluctant or slow to change, and a persistent surplus problem as the government tries, often futilely, to help the latter without creating a bonanza for the former.

Despite the success of the green revolution there are those who

choose to remain "cautiously pessimistic." Long ago Kipling
wrote:

> The end of the fight is a tombstone white
> with the name of the late deceased.
> And the epitaph drear: A fool lies here
> who tried to hustle the East.

Seemingly the East *is* hustling, but it is well to keep in mind the
people part of the problem as we get on with the technology.
Raymond Ewell put it very well:

The question is sometimes asked: If the United States can send a
man to the moon why can't we help India, Nigeria and Brazil to improve their agricultures? The answer is that improving the agricultures of India, Nigeria and Brazil is a more complicated problem than
sending a man to the moon. The problem of sending a man to the
moon can be solved by scientists and engineers using computers and
the vast store of scientific knowledge now available. Improving agriculture in the developing countries is more complicated because it
involves people and education and social changes—particularly since
it involves 2 billion people.

A 27-year-old fellow in Sao Paulo, Roque Gomes
Mariano, is strong and healthy while never eating any
vegetables or animal food but living exclusively on
gasoline, two liters a day, *O Globo* reported on Monday.
Brazil Herald

CHAPTER 11

Exotic Foods

Beyond the green revolution, what? Granting that it seems possible to feed the increasing population for some years to come, are there even more effective food production methods the hungry world can make use of? Indeed there are, although it is not likely that all these "blue sky" food schemes will bear fruit, in spite of the claims of their proponents.

Many exotic plans stem directly from science fiction; others seem to have been engendered in dreams brought on by too much rich food. Yet some that seem the wildest have been proposed by serious scientific thinkers on the subject. It may be difficult to separate the wheat from the chaff among this hodgepodge of ideas that abound both in the pages of learned journals and Sunday supplements, but some can be written off quickly.

One proposed solution to the food problem is to breed smaller people. Nature has for some time been doing that for us in food-short lands, but whether or not science can intentionally dwarf the human race—or if it should try—is a question you can put to your conscience. There is a nutty appeal in the idea of the minihuman, however, including potential alleviation of overcrowding, the saving of material in smaller houses and auto-mobiles, and so on. A grisly proposal going in somewhat the same direction is voluntary amputation and replacement of limbs with artificial ones. A symbolic feature of Bernard Wolfe's wild novel *Limbo*, such a literal paring down of the population would seem to appeal only to sadistic surgeons and the manufacturers of prosthetics.

There are tongue-in-cheek suggestions that we take a page from nature's book and revert to cannibalism—à la Swift's *Modest Proposal*. There is probably some human consumption of humans going on in the world today, but the idea is unlikely to catch on on a broad scale. For one thing, man has more DDT residue in his tissues than the FDA accepts in foodstuffs!

Some big-thinkers, bypassing all stopgap or intermediate solu-tions, blithely suggest that we metamorphize man into an "inde-pendent animal," a hybrid retaining the powers of locomotion and sensory perception while regaining the ability to convert sunlight, air, and water into carbohydrates. There have been re-ported cases of humans who subsisted on air and sunshine, but these people usually have something more solid up their sleeves than solar rays. There *is* a certain beauty to this method in that it combines sunbathing and snacking into a single pleasure! For those averse to nudity and outdoor living, perhaps an analogous power pack, able to be plugged into a wall socket, could be de-signed for recharging calories the way we pump energy back into a storage battery.

An old standby, the food pill, lingers on, not only in science-fiction tales but also in serious but misguided proposals for dietary sufficiency. We *could* switch to pills right now—if we were will-ing to swig down a pound or two of them a day, with or without sugar coating. Twentieth-century man possesses a Stone Age body that requires about as much input of food as ever. Much as we may hate to admit it, we also need ample roughage to keep our intestinal parasites happy and working for us. Nothing short of drastic surgical modification is going to change that picture, so we had best forget the pill approach—except perhaps to *lose* weight.

Solving two problems with a single solution, Dr. Richard L. Meier of the University of Michigan proposes huge floating cities as a twenty-first-century answer to both food and population problems. Many people have already taken to lakes, rivers, and even the sea in various craft. As cities begin to coalesce into megalopolises, the floating island proponents argue that man will have to build out over the water. Cities of 50,000 and more are envisioned, taking advantage of an abundance of real estate, clear skies above, and ample water and food below. Power would be produced by "sea thermal energy plants," the theory of which has long been known and demonstrated on a pilot basis. Water could be desalinated in the same plants, and oxygen extracted from the water using already-known techniques. Food could be grown on the sea or in it, bringing "mariculture" into its own, with men right on the marine range to manage the process.

In a poetic reversal of the manna-from-heaven solution that fed ancient Israelites hungry in the wilderness, some dreamers have suggested that man emigrate *into* the heavens and find a home and food on another planet. Appealing as this proposal might be to space nuts, it is not one of the more practical solutions to the food problem.

The French weekly *L'Express* in 1962 polled "experts" on the prognosis for man and food by the turn of the century. Here is the delightful conclusion reached:

> By the year 2000 all food will be completely synthetic. Agriculture and fisheries will have become superfluous. The world's population will by then have increased fourfold but will have stabilized. Sea water and ordinary rocks will yield all the necessary metals. Disease, as well as famine, will have been eliminated; and universal hygienic inspection and control will have been introduced. The problems of energy production will by then be completely resolved.

Concerned authorities rightly have little patience with such wave-of-the-hand solutions and see small hope in panaceas ex-

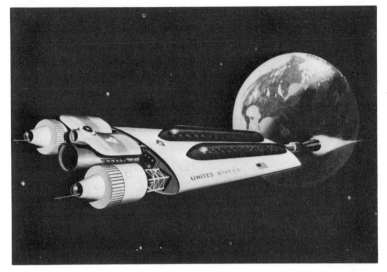

One way to beat overpopulation? Experts point out that emigration to other planets would be fantastically expensive as a solution to crowding.
NASA

pressed in purple prose. But perhaps we tend to be too pessimistic of the efficacy of dreams, too stodgy and tradition bound in our approaches to finding the additional food that may be needed. N. W. Pirie, the British expert on food, gives the FAO a general pat on the back but adds in an article in *Scientific American*, October 1965: ". . . one can deplore its equally persistent tendency to denigrate every unorthodox approach to the problem. . . . Early man lived precariously and in many parts of the world he spent a life of hardship in fertile areas of unrealized potential." Pirie's point is that perhaps there is likewise far more potential today than we realize, since we are generally as conditioned to our limiting traditions as early man was to his. Pirie himself has some highly imaginative ideas, as we shall see. There are many other scientists who think that even the green revolution is grindingly slow and that the only real progress will come from quantum jumps. The *Bulletin of the Atomic Scientists* in September 1965 editorialized:

. . . small and slow increases in food production are accompanied by a proportionate increase in the population . . .
Conventional methods of increasing food production, for example through agriculture and fisheries, cannot be expanded rapidly enough to provide this critical increase. Too many people are involved, and in many places the profound social changes required cannot be brought about quickly. We must turn from agriculture to the production of food by synthesis. Synthesis of large quantities of food that are basically identical with natural food can be achieved by relatively small numbers of people using readily available raw materials in facilities that can be set up and duplicated almost anywhere in the world.

Perhaps this, too, comes under the heading of twist-of-the-wrist, the too-easy solution. Before we tackle the synthesis of food we should cut our teeth on some less far-out solutions. Let's begin with the supercharging of conventional agriculture.

Easing the Water Crisis

An earlier chapter noted that the Scientific Advisory Committee believed irrigation could add 200 million acres to the world's arable soil. But if there is already a water shortage—and there definitely is, even in the United States—how can we irrigate more lands? Here is a paradox of shortage in the midst of plenty, but it may be possible to find some answers.

There is a lot of water on our planet, as is obvious in photos taken of it from space. Earth is, in fact, mostly water, with some 100 billion gallons for each of us humans on a prorated basis. Even a doubling of population will still leave us plenty of water. Not all of this is fresh water, of course, but there is a billion gallons of that for each one of us. The trouble is, we are at present polluting it faster in some places than nature can purify it. So we must increasingly distill or otherwise desalt water that is not now fit for use.

There are a number of different approaches for this, including nuclear-fueled distillation plants that use heat to evaporate water by the same principle as the crudest stills man has ever built; ionic-membrane systems that "filter" out impurities; "osmotic" or pressure systems that do about the same thing; and solar energy stills, a few fairly large-scale versions of which are operating in various parts of the world, including Mexico, Greece, Australia, the United States, and Israel. Because the sun's heat is relatively "low grade," or diffuse, it is doubtful that solar energy can ever be called on to produce fresh water for conventional agriculture economically, since water is used in such quantities in "dirt farming." However, we shall shortly look at some unconventional farming techniques in which solar energy may be used.

Many experts are pessimistic about being able to desalinate water by any method cheaply enough for agricultural uses, geared as farming is to water at a few dollars an acre-foot. One glum researcher expressed desalination economics in this graphic fashion: Evaporation of seawater requires about half an inch of oil per acre to produce enough water to irrigate *one acre*. Forty tons of oil a year would thus produce food for only one or two people. There may be better ways of using oil for food.

Much irrigation water is surplus, and runs off the low end of the field. It may be feasible to recycle this water, with some purification in the process. Santee, California, is among the communities that have already learned that even sewage can be purified and reused for recreational purposes and as domestic water. Some waste water is now sold as irrigation for farming. Sewage, in addition to harmful bacteria, contains useful bacteria, nitrogen, carbon dioxide, and other constituents beneficial to plants. It may prove practicable to irrigate and fertilize fields with sewage and to fertilize estuaries for fish farming in the same manner, an optimistic note amidst all the dire pollution warnings. Brno, Czechoslovakia, Munich, Germany, and Melbourne, Australia, are among those cities already using sewage to irrigate agricultural lands.

Much protest has also been made about the "thermal pollution" of our water, and rightly so, for slight temperature variations can be harmful to aquatic life. Fish are killed by water only a few degrees above temperatures they have become accustomed to. However, heat is energy, and the thought has occurred that it might be possible to turn thermal pollution to good use in agriculture. Some estimates indicate that 25 percent of our surface water supply will be used in power plant heat-exchangers by 1985. The Atomic Energy Commission has a proposal for a warm-water irrigation project, using this effluent. The $2.6 million required is not yet forthcoming, but the Eugene, Oregon, Water and Electric Board is funding a $475,000 demonstration, sprinkling warm water to stimulate plant growth and prevent destruction of trees by frost. Preliminary tests, using electric wire stimulation, indicate that corn and string beans benefit from heating but that alfalfa, soybeans, and lima beans do not.

The Weather-Makers

A most challenging idea is that of weather control, including rainmaking and generally better conditions for farming and other agricultural pursuits. For many years a few men have attempted to manipulate the weather and make it rain for crops or stay clear for horse races and picnics. It has been proved that seeding of clouds *can* increase precipitation, although the technique is by no means practical as yet. Some fear that large-scale weather is so complex and so inexorably governed by factors over which man has no control that weather-changing of a nature to benefit farming cannot ever succeed. Be that as it may, there are a number of weather-making firms busy throughout the world today, convinced and convincing others that they are preventing hail, putting out forest fires, and providing rain for farming and for filling reservoirs. United States Government officials have guardedly predicted adding appreciable amounts to rainfall basins through artificial modification of the weather.

Tapping the "rivers in the sky," as a former Secretary of the

Interior put it, is one of the most exciting of the far-out food-producing ideas yet advanced. Ironically, the idea dates back to ancient times, when magicians were commissioned to end droughts.

Remote Sensing

Another challenging technique, this one a product of the space age, is "remote sensing," monitoring the progress of plant—and animal—life from high in the air. In just a few years this eye-in-the-sky technique, first used for military surveillance by spy aircraft, has become a bright hope of food-planners, among many others. Thus far it has demonstrated its ability to detect ripe crops, plant diseases, wasted water, new ground water sources, freshwater springs emptying into the ocean, the exact location of the Gulf Stream and other currents, schools of fish, snow cover and depth, salinity and temperature of water, moisture content of soil, forest fires otherwise undetected, subterranean coal and peat fires, soil drainage, the pollution of estuaries, lakes, rivers, and oceans, and many other important factors in food production.

One stumbling block to implementation of remote sensing is the fear that aerial "snooping" may work to the disadvantage of some; in fact constant disclaimers of any evil intent have been deemed necessary since the first mention was made of remote sensing as an aid to stocking the world's food larders.

Pie in the Sky

One of the wilder ideas to come from the age of space, as we have said, is that of emigrating from earth. The price per head for round trips to the moon via Apollo ought to indicate the high cost of this food-saving dodge. In fact, Garrett Hardin devastated the whole notion long ago when he pointed out that to move 170 million emigrants a year (assuming a "full earth" of 10 billion by about the year 2020) to Alpha Centauri would require 1.7 mil-

This photograph made with panchromatic infrared film shows a brown soft scale infested orchard here. Detection of only the most severe areas of infestation is possible on regular color or on panchromatic film since all trees appear fairly dark. On infrared film, however, healthy trees show high reflectance and infected trees appear darker.
USDA

lion spaceships a year, built at a cost of $300 million each. Actually, since it would take them 350 years to get there, by which time each craft would carry 2,000 passengers rather than the starting lineup of 100, it would be necessary to build 2,000-passenger craft at a cost of several billion or more per ship. And stewardesses would have to stock an amazing quantity of in-flight meals.

Hardin seemed to be stacking the deck against space flight by setting such a distant goal, but even Mars or Venus would pose some impossible logistical problems. It may be that the only food help we will get from the space effort will come as fallout from space nutrition research, although thus far such diets seem little different from novelties available at the corner market.

Technician prepares to eat a fruit bar in Gemini Capsule.
NASA

There have been some interesting "closed-ecology" experiments carried on for NASA, however. After early work that suggested such Epicurean delights as chickens fed on bones, feathers, and entrails plus algae grown on human waste, "bioregeneration" by hydrogen bacteria was introduced by Martin aerospace scientists in 1965. These "hydrogenomonads" subsist on hydrogen and multiply without benefit of photosynthesis, guaranteeing around-the-clock production. Tests indicated that twenty to thirty liters of such a suspension, or soup, could support one man, converting his carbon dioxide and producing enough oxygen and protein to sustain him. We shall meet bacteria similar to the hydrogen-eaters in some terrestrial food-production settings.

Prior to the moon landings, scientist Willard Libby suggested that the lunar soil might be rich in organic materials, and, even though Libby's notion doesn't seem to have been confirmed, many experts still talk of farming the moon. N. W. Pirie has suggested that leafy plants would do well even on the moon. As might be expected, all this sounded as lunatic to most people as green cheese, and British science journals referred to it jestingly as "pie in the sky." Rather than wait for help from space, it might be well to get back down to the earth from which our sustenance still springs.

The Plastic Farm

Despite much hope on several fronts, the water problem is far from solved. The other side of the coin from purifying water to a tolerance acceptable to plants is to select or breed plants with a tolerance for saline or otherwise polluted water. Some strides have been made in this direction, particularly in Israel. Another approach is to grow plants with less water. Actually, the natural "transpiration" process seems most inefficient, and work is in progress to develop leafy plants that waste less water than the 98 percent they now do.

The ultimate seems to be farms "sealed in plastic." Controlled environments, with carbon dioxide added to the air—perhaps even pressurized air at that—with an optimum temperature maintained, nutrients added, and with little water lost in the process, are well past the laboratory stage.

Far from being a space-age concept, closed-environment growing of plants had its beginnings in "hydroponics," which Webster defines as "the growing of plants in nutrient solutions with or without an inert medium to provide mechanical support." Although hydroponics flowered briefly during World War II, on such places as Ascension Island, a tiny volcanic island in the South Atlantic that supported little vegetation, it was actually first practiced in the laboratory in 1699. However, until recently it

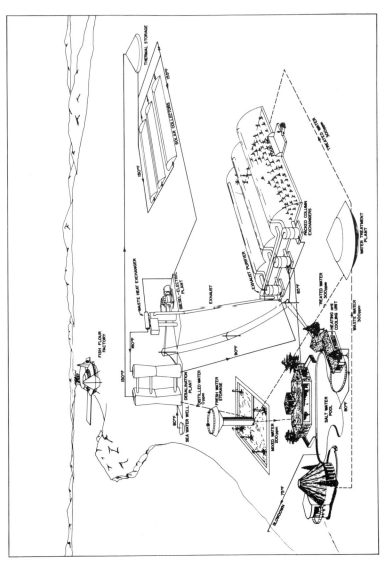

Idealized schematic of system for production of power, water, and food for coastal desert community.
University of Arizona

has not amounted to much more than an experimental or hobby technique. Now there are a number of seemingly promising installations in various parts of the world.

Carl Hodges, of the University of Arizona in Tucson, described an interesting project at the 1966 Symposium on Water Production Using Nuclear Energy, at Tucson:

An interest in the general world food and water problem had led the Solar Energy Laboratory staff to speculate also on the possibilities of producing food, particularly with the use of sea water, although it was not hoped that the plants could be grown in direct contact with the sea water. It is well known that, for their nutrition, plants require less than two per cent of the water they absorb and transpire to the atmosphere. It was felt that if they could be grown in a fully enclosed environment, using simple vapor and humidity exchange mechanisms between sea water and plant atmosphere, a productive horticulture could be maintained on an extremely small quantity of fresh water. A number of different experiments have been performed testing this hypothesis. It has been demonstrated that this is entirely feasible, the only requirement being the maintenance of carbon dioxide concentration in the closed atmosphere. Calculations indicate that this can be easily handled from the diesel engine exhaust with sea water scrubbing and a low-temperature catalyst for removing objectionable gases from the exhaust. A number of different crops have been tested and the feasibility of, for example, tomato productivity above the level of 100 tons per acre per year has been demonstrated.

Staff members are now at work on a full-scale closed-environment agriculture system for the tiny sheikdom of Abu Dhabi on the Persian Gulf. This will provide food and fresh water, both of which are in short supply locally in Abu Dhabi. Arthur Godfrey is sponsoring a hydroponics operation in Hawaii, and the United Nations has also taken an interest in closed-environment farming; it is reported to be providing funds for a pilot installation of plastic farming engineered by Hydroculture, Inc., of Phoenix, Arizona. The UN testing will be done in Lebanon. Meanwhile, Hydroculture has an apparently successful commercial venture in operation near Phoenix, marketing premium quality tomatoes under the trade name of Magic Garden.

In this operation, tomatoes are grown at the rate of about 1 million pounds a year in forty greenhouses, each measuring 26 by 128 feet. Steel-framed and covered with plastic, the greenhouses have concrete floors, with gravel serving as the plant bed. Water and nutrients are automatically fed to the plants, which grow eight feet tall on vertical cords. Temperature is controlled to 85 degrees F during the day and 65 degrees F at night. According to spokesmen, each mature tomato plant produces thirty pounds of marketable tomatoes a year, compared with eight to ten pounds on conventional plants. Eight 26- by 128-foot greenhouses produce as much as from four to eight acres of land.

Cucumbers and chard are also being grown in this experiment, and, in another chamber, called the Magic Meadow, grass is cultivated for feeding livestock. One pound of oat or barley seed produces seven to nine pounds of grass eight to ten inches high in a week, with the result that the Magic Meadow yields a crop of 500 to 600 pounds a day. There are a number of similar installations around the country, and among those using and approving the system are the San Diego Zoo and a number of animal breeders.

According to an advertising brochure, ". . . the next step predicted by experts may benefit householders of the next generation, who may for under $500 purchase a unit no larger than a conventional refrigerator, that will grow all the lettuce, tomatoes and other vegetables for a family's needs."

Whether or not this glowing prediction—and perhaps a matching miniaturized home animal farm—will come to pass for the next generation remains to be seen. The idea is especially intriguing in an age when it seems that only gigantic farming operations can succeed. Growing crops under plastic, free from drought, flood, storm, pests—and pesticides!—certainly has advantages to be exploited.

New Bottles for Old Vines

Some agricultural scientists feel that there is too much "man with the hoe" philosophy in farming and that we are not doomed to till the soil by brute force for all time. "Chemical tillage" is suggested as an alternative, and promising work has been done in applying such preparations to the soil instead of churning and deviling it with plows, rakes, cultivators, discs, and harrows. The agricultural chemical "paraquat" (trade name, Gramoxone), used experimentally in Europe, Canada, Australia, and the United States, has proved that soil in "chemical fallow" held 40 percent more rain than soil conventionally cultivated to control weeds. Yields following chemical fallow have been reported as 20 percent higher than for other methods.

In general, farmers deplore the advance of blacktop, or asphalt. But one suggested farming technique calls for blacktopping agricultural land, the difference from conventional parking-lot paving being that asphalt in the farming technique is applied two feet *below* the surface, to hold water and heat better than natural soil. Michigan State University researchers have laid test plots of asphalt at a cost of about $225 an acre. Half an inch thick, and in thirty-four-inch widths overlapped several inches, the asphalt is expected to have a life of fifteen years and crop yield increases are estimated from 20 to 100 percent. In a similar method, rose growers and others have laid tar paper, prepunched for insertion of seed, in the fields. As does the asphalt, tar paper holds down weeds, conserves water, and increases heat in the soil.

Artificial light has also been used for such plants as strawberries, cucumbers, and tomatoes, as well as flowers. In Ireland 400-watt mercury fluorescent lamps are used. This is supplemental lighting, but some all-artificial-light experiments have been done. The Dutch flowered tulips, narcissus, and hyacinths—which don't photosynthesize—in the early 1950s. At Shinfield, Reading, in

The dugong, an aquatic mammal suggested by some as an additional source of meat.
USDA

England, tomatoes have tripled their growth under artificial light. The next step would seem to be to add artificial light to hydroponic installations and thus extend the growing season.

New Crops and Creatures

Beyond new concepts and new environments, there are still other possibilities. Science has improved the plants and animals we use for food, and this improvement seems bound to continue. While work continues with the single-celled, fast-growing algae, which still retain some of their initial glamour (although George Borgstrom points out that the Aztecs harvested the stuff and prepared a kind of bread from it, and that some Sahara tribes near

The leaves of the water hyacinth, which flourishes in many places, have been suggested as a source of food.
USDA

Lake Chad still do!), selected leafy plants are now being suggested as prospects for new foods. Here Pirie is joined by Rockefeller Foundation people in pointing out that such plants are high in protein and may have even more productive capability per acre than algae. Pirie also notes that algae have marine competition, too, such as the water hyacinth, which grows so fast that it has become a menace to waterways. Adapting some such plant for food production could serve a twofold purpose and thus be more economic. In the back of some minds is the dream of Jack and the beanstalk, brought up to date and put to practice with the growth-enhancing "gibberellins" discovered by the Japanese. Plants, unlike animals, have the potential for almost unlimited growth.

Tissue Culture

Another interesting prospect is that of growing plant and animal tissue in laboratories instead of in the natural outside environment. Hydroponics and other such controlled-environment methods are but half a step toward the true tissue culture process. Demonstrated long ago by Dr. Alexis Carrel, laboratory culture of animal tissue in nutrient broth is accomplished fact. Carrel in the 1930s and 1940s kept bits of chicken heart alive and well and growing in containers. In a living plant or animal a cell is nourished by environment and a complex physicochemical system. In tissue culture in the lab, environment and nutrients are both provided artificially, and the cellular material grows and grows and grows. Pilot programs aim at factory production of meat and plant tissue in a very carefully controlled and enhanced atmosphere.

In their science fiction novel, *The Space Merchants*, Frederik Pohl and C. M. Kornbluth describe a food factory of the future that uses the tissue culture technique. Ironically, workers meet in a secret hideaway carved inside "Chicken Little," as they call the monstrous glob of blindly growing fowl tissue, to plan a revolution! No such subversion occurred during pilot operations at Melpar, Inc., with tissue culture under government contract; it would have required tiny revolutionaries, for one thing. The goal was tomatoes without the leaves, vine, or roots; pork chops produced without the pig; and perhaps square eggs and potatoes for more convenient packaging.

Much emphasis has also been placed on the laboratory culture of nerve tissue, cartilage, and other such living material for use in skin grafts, transplants, and so on. There is even guarded talk of growing whole organs as implant replacements for victims of disease or accident. Supplying food is a less dramatic but no less important application of tissue culture.

The Food-Spinners

Each year millions of tons of potential high-protein food is wasted through nonuse of oilseeds like soybeans, peanuts, cottonseed, and sunflowers. Unlike algae, whose cell walls are indigestible and must be separated out or digested with enzymes, oilseed cake poses no difficult problems. True, there is a constituent called "gossypol" that must be handled properly, but experimental work in Guatemala, Mysore, and at Rothamsted Experimental Station in England indicates that oilseed cake makes a good protein-rich additive. The real problem is the inertia of human taste. "Grandpa wouldn't have dreamed of eating such stuff," is the complaint, "and neither will I."

It is the old story of leading the horse to water but not being able to get him to drink. The nutritive value of a new food is far from enough to assure its acceptance; the product must also be carefully designed to match cultural patterns of food consumption. For example, fish and shellfish powders or the like should do well in parts of Asia that dote on fermented fish sauce. Oilseed additives could also supplement diets of gruel or curry. It is argued that a nation selling refrigerators to Eskimos, and Cokes and baby food to Ugandans (42 percent of them were feeding their babies canned food by 1959), should also be able to market wholesome food substitutes. Yet Corn Products International couldn't give away Enriched Maizena, and Quaker Oats asked AID for a $150,000 subsidy to help push its Incaparina.

While many authorities are ready by now to consign all food supplements to animal-feeding chores, there is one ray of hope in the so-called meat "analogues." General Mills has been in the forefront of this food development, and we now can buy the results in some markets. Briefly, an analogue is a product similar to a natural food. General Mills "spins" high-purity oilseed protein into monofilaments, or single threads, to provide what they describe as a "textural basis," although "textile" seems to be the word. Oilseed meal of 55 percent protein is upgraded to almost pure protein, spun much like nylon or other synthetics, and then combined with wheat gluten, egg albumin, and vegetable or animal fats. Flavors and coloring are added to simulate the taste and appearance of whatever the analoguers seek to duplicate. Hamburger, ham, chicken à la king, bacon, and seafood are among the "meats" produced, and this only scratches the surface of the possibilities.

According to General Mills the versatility of analogue foods is almost unlimited, ranging from zero cholesterol foods, kosher meats, hot dogs, fruits, vegetables or nut meats. Tenderness and texture are under complete control. Such "engineering" of foods may offend the purist or the nature faddist. But it is honest engineering, and General Mills deplores the word "synthetic" in reference to its new foods, claiming they are not substitute, synthetic, or imitation any more than are cheese, sausage, or spaghetti.

As dogs have demonstrated in TV commercials, even their sensitive taste and smell can be fooled by meat analogues. More importantly for humans, tests in Guatemala with analogue foods demonstrated that children recovered from kwashiorkor when fed on them. Further tests with volunteers showed no harmful effects from six months of analogue food diet.

General Mills points out that even the hamburger analogue, which they consider the most unfavorable economic comparison, can be produced for about half the cost of beef hamburger and provides more protein. In the offing is the use of FPC and other protein concentrates with the spun oilseed fiber. In the offing, too, if history is any indicator, is resistance from the natural meat industry, and from consumers who will claim that if God intended us to eat analogues he would have endowed Eden with monofilament-spinning equipment instead of animals.

Chicken Feed

There's an old story about a farmer who got his horse to eat
excelsior by fitting him with green glasses so he'd think it was
hay. Unfortunately the horse died about the time he got used to
the substitute food. The story is truly old, for we are now to the
point of using cellulose to feed animals without even offering
them colored glasses.

Hogs, cattle and poultry have been fed fish meal for a long
time. There have also been experiments with activated sludge as
feed for sheep, pigs, and ducks in space-food experiments. Cows
have been fed waste paper, made tastier with some molasses, and
Marcus Bishop writing in *The Scientist Speculates* has suggested
that the protozoan *Trichonymphia*, which lives inside the termite
and digests wood for it, be introduced into our meat-producing
animals—which could then graze on trees, trunk and all! Larger
termites would seem to be an alternative suggestion, to be eaten
directly as food.

More seriously, there is a possibility of feeding cattle on waste
cellulose from the dump. We produce about three pounds of such
trash per person a day, and General Electric is among those con-
ducting research into using bacteria to convert this waste into
protein. Maintained at 130 to 180 degrees F, a disposal plant such
as is being considered would kill off disease bacteria and viruses,
while sewage sludge would serve as a nutrient for the process.
Dr. W. Dexler Bellamy of G.E. has studied 140 colonies of
bacteria and isolated pure strains that digest cellulose readily,
reproduce quickly, and produce a biomass containing a high percentage of protein. Bacterial conversion of cellulose by ruminants
is the model for this process.

Many hungry nations produce sugar for export. The Oxford
Committee for Famine Relief suggests that turning this into protein would be much wiser. It was once thought that no more
than about 15 percent of an animal's diet should be sugar; now as

much as 73 percent molasses had been fed to them, supplemented with urea. The point is, meat sells for up to ten times what sugar does. And experiments show that three times as many cattle can be fattened on a field of sugar beets or cane than on maize.

Petroleum Protein

In an earlier chapter the analogy was made between food and the fuel in a gasoline tank. Heading this chapter is a humorous item on gasoline as human food. Interestingly, gasoline and other fuels are organic, that is, they contain hydrocarbons. Turn that word around, add oxygen and we have carbohydrates, which are food. Despite the Brazilian's claim for his liquid diet, no one is yet subsisting on gasoline or diesel fuel—except bacteria and fungi. However, these life forms *are* in turn producing yeast, which is then fed to animals to produce human food!

The fuel for our mechanical engines may thus be used one day to fuel the human machine as well. Not yet usable on a commercial basis, neither is protein from petroleum a science-fiction idea. In fact, the Société Française de Petroles has set up a pilot plant in France that has turned out quantities of fungi suitable for food, the fungi themselves being fed mainly on a diet of petroleum.

Actually the growing of fungi for food is an ancient practice, and man has raised yeast for a long time to use in bread-making, brewing, and the making of wine and alcohol. In nature wild yeasts are believed carried by insects from soil to fruits, where they activate the fermentation process. Yeast is rich in vitamins and has been used for nourishment and to treat certain ailments. Commercial yeast is grown on molasses and produces vitamins and proteins comparable to those of animal flesh. Instead of doubling their weight over a period of months or years, the yeast microorganisms—which reproduce by budding—accomplish this gain in five hours or less.

Microbiologists at Mobil's Princeton laboratory. The powder on the left is the protein equivalent of 1.2 pounds of steak and can be produced in a few hours from the amount of petroleum liquid shown on the right.
Photograph by Mobil Oil Corporation, U.S.A., issued by FAO, Rome

Molasses itself is a food, and using it as a substrate for yeast competes with other uses for molasses—such as feeding cattle. Scientists wondered if petroleum, a hydrocarbon, could be substituted for carbohydrates. It has long been known that bacteria do grow in oil, for refiners had become interested in microbial action in connection with the dewaxing of oil. Bacteria had been found in refining tanks, in asphalt roads, in the plumbing of oil plants, and even in aircraft fuel tanks, where additives are required to prevent their growth. German biologist Felix Just reported in 1952 that he had grown yeast on pure hydrocarbons of the paraffin family, and a few years later the French research group set up a project at Lavera. Work began there about 1957. The

United States and various European and Asian countries followed suit.

While the process of growing yeast on carbohydrates is a simple one, the petroleum process posed some sticky chemical and technical problems. No water is present in oil, and neither is oxygen. So the oil had to be "suspended" in water, and kept in this mixed state by constant stirring. Oxygen was supplied by bubbling it through the suspension. Another problem was the great amount of heat generated by the growing bacteria—three times that present in normal growth of carbohydrates. For this reason a cooling system had to be added. There were offsetting advantages, however. Yeast was produced twice as fast as by the normal method, and under ideal conditions a pound of oil could produce a pound of yeast—an efficiency of protein production of 100 percent. Here were two great incentives: rapid growth and highly efficient production of protein.

Thus far the workers at Lavera had used pure hydrocarbons, such as Just had used. Now they tried various fractions of crude oils. As expected, the aromatic hydrocarbons were hostile to bacterial growth—the aromatics were used to fight bacteria in fuel systems. But a gas-oil fraction between kerosene and lubricating oil was found to produce good results. Indeed, experiments with various microorganisms indicated that a wide variety of protein products could be produced, as workers in antibiotic production had already established in that different application. A most useful by-product also resulted from the use of the selected fraction. Since the yeast fed mainly on paraffin, the oil was at the same time being further refined, producing what is called a "No. 2" fuel oil in the process and raising the value of the original fraction. (In 1966 Pittsburgh Coal Project reported growing yeasts on coal-tar paraffins. Pure hydrocarbons gave a 72 percent yield; carbon sources from the "Fischer-Tropsch" process 41 percent, and some tar fractions a 29 percent yield.)

Although growing yeast on oil hardly resembles farming, analogous processes are involved. For example, nitrogen is added in the form of ammonia salts, and phosphorus and potassium fertilizers are also provided. About 50 percent of the yeast product is protein, differing in no essential way from protein produced by cattle, fish, chickens, plants, or sugar-grown yeast. In fact, the oil yeast was found to be particularly high in the important amino acid lysine.

The British Petroleum Company assisted the French workers in their project, and became so interested it also set up projects in the Paris area, a research and development center at Grangemouth, Scotland, and a field location in Nigeria to study the effects of feeding cattle on the oil-grown yeast. The yeast has been used as an additive in many foods, including fish sauces, and is also packaged as a dry powder much like skimmed milk to be used in cooking and baking. While no great commercial success has attended the efforts of the French and British researchers, the potential of using petroleum for food is intriguing. As the Lavera people pointed out, 40 million tons of crude oil could yield 20 million tons of proteins a year, double the total annual production of protein at that time (1965).

Forty million tons is a tiny fraction of the world's output of about 1.25 *billion* tons (1965). Oil is relatively cheap, and stable in price because of widespread demand. Because there are some 700 refineries, distributed in nearly all countries, and because the oil industry has the chemical and technical know-how through producing a variety of oil products and by-products, it would be feasible to set up yeast-producing operations on a global basis.

An editorial in the *Bulletin of the Atomic Scientists* in 1965 came up with a different set of figures but endorsed the idea:

. . . protein deficiency (from 8 to 20 grams daily) could be made up at a cost of about $4 billion. This represents the production of about 10 million metric tons of essential amino acids at a cost of about $4 a kilo, or about $18 per person a year.

To do this with petroleum would require about 18 kilos of petroleum per person a year. Present consumption is about 104 kilos per person [for energy production] and rising at about 10 percent a year.

Eighteen kilograms is about 40 pounds. Earlier we noted that 40 *tons* of oil would desalinate only enough water to feed one or two people in conventional agriculture.

While some authorities claimed it would be at least ten years before petroleum yeast food was available for humans, and that such protein was still short of conventional animal protein, British Petroleum in 1968 reported feeding gas-oil yeast to pigs and poultry. In a test, a yeast-fed pig was eaten by 250 people. Of these, 170 thought they could taste the difference; half of these preferred the yeast, and half the control pig. The other 80 tasted no difference in the samples. Perhaps Roque Gomes Mariano, the gasoline drinker in the chapter heading, *could* subsist on two liters of gasoline a day—if he first filtered it through a batch of fungi and a litter of pigs!

The Real Synthetics

As General Mills has pointed out, their analogue foods are not synthetic, since they use natural plant materials as a basis. Soybean meats are thus a long, long way from foods produced by chemists instead of by nature, artificial as they may taste.

Writing in *Road to Abundance*, J. Rosin and M. Eastman in 1953 predicted synthetic foods:

Meat proteins, which are now the most expensive of all staple foods, and available in sufficient quantities only to a small part of the world's population, will then be available to everybody at a nominal cost. The systematic protein undernourishment of the majority of mankind will cease. Millions of cattle raisers and packing-industry employees will be replaced by a few chemical operators. The disgrace of slaughterhouses will disappear from our cities, and one will have to go to a zoological garden to see a cow. Our grandchildren will hardly believe that we were so barbaric and primitive that we had to eat cadavers of dead animals in order to keep alive.

Fresh from a steak dinner, it is difficult to concede the "disgrace" of slaughterhouses. Cattle-raisers may not want to be replaced by a "few chemical operators." So it is fortunate that we will not stop eating animal cadavers in the near future. However, drugs, resins, and dyes have long been synthesized, and some amino acids are now synthesized commercially, methionine and lysine for example, and the latter very cheaply. Dr. Nevin Scrimshaw, head of the Department of Nutrition and Food Science at M.I.T., points out that the simple hydrocarbon, 1-3 butanediol, costing fourteen cents a pound in carload lots, has a caloric density of six calories per gram and is used as animal feed.

Another approach suggested at NASA is the direct chemical synthesis of carbohydrates. Several methods could produce polymers of formaldehyde (CH_2O), the essential formula of carbohydrate, which would be mixed with protein. One problem this faces, however, is assimilation of small molecules by humans used to eating natural "giant" molecules.

While not advocating a crash program for synthetic foods, because of high costs of production and a lack of need for them now, Scrimshaw does suggest that they will be significant by the end of the century—which checks with the Rosin and Eastman timetable, coincidentally! We may have to go to the zoo to reminisce—or to get a real steak—in the year 2000.

We can manage for food without adopting the exotic methods set out in this chapter for some time to come. Should it prove possible to curb population increase, we may never have to call on techniques much different from those we now use. However, it is comforting to have these potential alternatives against the time when a quantum jump in food production becomes necessary.

Our earth is but a small star in the great universe. Yet of it we can make, if we choose, a planet unvexed by war, untroubled by hunger. . . .

> Prayer written by Stephen Vincent Benét and read by President Franklin D. Roosevelt to the United Nations (twenty-six nations fighting against the Axis powers in World War II) on Flag Day, 1942

CHAPTER 12

Can We Get There from Here?

Concern over the population explosion and global hunger is admirable, but many of those most agitated seem to understand the phenomena poorly. One book complains that earth cannot support the 3.5 billion now alive—then warns that if we aren't careful there will soon be *15 billion!* With such logic it is easy to get lost in Aristotelian thickets, and much of the problem is not logical anyhow. Emotion rules, not only in the conception of children but in attempts to solve the problems their birth brings on.

Understandably, there is frustration to the point of bitterness over the seeming lack of results in attempts to control population. An official of the Population Crisis Committee says: "Family planning means, among other things, that if we are going to multiply like rabbits, we should do it on purpose. One couple may plan to have three children; another couple may plan seven. In both cases, they are a cause of the population problem—not a solution to it."

ZPG exponent Dr. Paul Ehrlich deplores the fact that of 55,000 IUDs inserted in Hong Kong, 21,000 dropped out or were intentionally removed. He also says that to sterilize only the males in India who have already sired three or more children would keep 1,000 surgeons busy eight hours a day for eight years; meanwhile, the list of candidates for such operations grows daily.

The Fight Against Life

Ehrlich's ready answer is that we must immediately establish a crash program in the United States to limit our own "serious population explosion." Perhaps limit is not the correct word, since Ehrlich believes that 150 million is a reasonable level in this country. After we accomplish this first priority, he says we must then set up an international program with "tough and realistic policies" for dealing with the population crisis overall.

According to Ehrlich, the federal Population Commission must implement a four-point program: (1) tax penalties on larger families; (2) mandatory birth control education in schools; (3) permissive abortions; (4) forgetting of "death control" and "quality of life" until the quantity of life can be controlled.

For many environmentalists the standard answer is instant abortion. These are often conservationists who tend to point to nature as a model. Yet induced abortion in animals is unknown; no abortionists, legal or otherwise, ever set up shop in caves and dens. Animals *do* desert their young, however, and on occasion even eat them. Some young eat their parents, too, and adults eat mates, although such tactics hardly seem a profitable object lesson for the human race.

Let us not castigate ourselves more than we deserve. There may be no family-planner groups in populations of rabbits or lemmings, but for many years there have been a number of humans who have dedicated themselves to birth control, especially in this country. Indeed, no country, except for Sweden perhaps, has more diligently advocated birth control for the developing nations than has the United States. We have, as we have seen, spent millions of dollars in attempts to develop new techniques and to "sell" these techniques to the Indians, the Africans, the Latins, and others. Yet after all this sex education and all the effort and money spent on IUDs and bounties for vasectomy volunteers, what emerges as most used and most effective? None other than the old-fashioned condom. Or abortion, a method older than contraception.

For all the breast-beating and arm-flailing of birth-controllers, it is doubtful that any breakthroughs are imminent. The population avalanche was a long time in the making and it will be a long time in getting slowed down. Instead of indulging in bombast and pointless rhetoric, those concerned with population would do well to face the facts of life.

We have seen that in the United States population is not exploding. With the birthrate at an all-time low, efforts continue to bring it even lower. In 1970 the U.S. Senate voted a $1 billion, five-year population control program. This would include birth control clinics plus free contraceptives to all who want them. A new deputy assistant secretary for population affairs in the Department of Health, Education, and Welfare was also authorized.

It is within the realm of hope that before many decades we will be aiming toward maintaining a stable population instead of gearing ourselves to perpetual human inflation as well as inflation of the economic variety. But what of the developing nations, those in which famine has struck in the past, and may do so again? It is now painfully obvious that, barring miracle or catastrophe, population curbs are not going to stop the runaway growth in other countries for some time to come. The problem then lies in nourishing the newcomers along with those already here.

They Can't Be Saved!

As there are for population control, there are some harsh proposals for solving the hunger problem, too. Years ago Dr. Alfred Smee suggested that the Irish tragedy would take care of itself if no one intervened—apparently he meant that death would eliminate the starving excess. A century and a quarter later there are still such hardnoses with us who claim that we just can't get there from here unless we cut certain starving peoples adrift and forget them.

The theme of Paul and William Paddock's sensational book *Famine—1975* is a concept called "triage." Borrowing the term from military medicine, the Paddocks explain that the world's hungry must be considered in the way surgeons in the field categorize the wounded: (1) the can't-be-saved's, (2) the walking wounded, and (3) those who can be saved by immediate care.

In blunt terms the Paddocks say that we cannot hope to save the whole world, and must begin to face up to the uncomfortable choices left. Presently we ship food to 111 countries and dependencies under Public Law 480, and in so doing we spread our aid potential too thin. What is the point in prolonging the misery of the "can't-be-saved"? Why help those who can by effort take care of themselves? Instead, we must concentrate on those "who can be saved by immediate care." Who are these fortunate ones? Pakistan and Tunisia are among these selected by the Paddocks for continued help. Libya and The Gambia are examples of walking wounded who will pull through on their own. But India, Egypt, and Haiti are past hope. They can't be saved.

Thomas H. Huxley, in *Joseph Priestley*, addressed himself to the implications of widespread hunger some time ago: "Becky Sharp's acute remark that it is not difficult to be virtuous on ten thousand a year has its applications to nations: it is futile to expect a hungry and squalid population to be anything but violent and gross." Actually, Thackeray had Becky say five thousand pounds, but Huxley's point is obvious, as well as currently applicable.

There is much talk that developed nations *must* help the underdeveloped or risk war; that starvation breeds revolution and leads to conflict. This hardly seems a realistic appraisal of the situation, since people starving to death are hardly in condition to make war on those better off, particularly if the "haves" are

Developing countries will continue to need help from others who are better off.
USDA

thousands of miles removed from the scene—and especially when it requires sophisticated and highly expensive weapons to wage modern war.

Assuming hundreds of millions of Asians to be starving, it would hardly benefit their leaders to develop nuclear weapons that would destroy the developed West, or even make it possible to take over those countries, since all the agricultural resources in them could not possibly feed the hungry East.

To those who worry about uprisings in the doomed nations, the Paddocks point out that ". . . a nation in the chaos of famine poses no threat of disaster to us." They then go on to rationalize their surely hard-to-reach decision: "Triage satisfies the humanitarians in saving the greatest number of lives, patriots in safeguarding the economic stability of the United States, diplomats in safeguarding political, strategic, and economic interests, and realists, in keeping goals within the limits of our own resources."

Even to consider so ruthless a plan as "triage" must be a bitter pill for anyone—including surely the Paddocks. But swallow it

they do in all deadly seriousness. They are certain that we have
no other choice, for fear of our own destruction as the starving
world goes down.

The Paddocks note that only four nations are food sufficient:
the United States, Canada, Australia, and Argentina. But among
these only the United States can be counted on to give food to
the hungry. The others will sell it—at going prices. Senator Allen
Ellender has agreed, making this statement in congressional hearings in August 1969 on the food problem:

> We tried to get food for India. I understand we went to Australia.
> They said, we have no more, we sold it to China. We went to Canada.
> They, too, said, we have no more, we sold it to China. We went to
> the United Kingdom and asked for assistance in behalf of the Indians.
> What did they offer? To carry a few hundred thousand bushels of
> wheat that they will get from us. We are the only ones now that
> have the wheat and the grain in any amount, and my guess is that
> when it is all over, you will find that Uncle Sam is footing most of the
> bill, as we have been doing in the past.

Another legislator voiced the same opinion, pointing out that he
had been told by foreign diplomats, "This is surplus and we do
you a favor by taking it!"

The Paddocks' comment is:

> Don't speak of the "strategy of the well-fed nations" in the plural.
> The record shows that only the U.S.A. will give free grain in ade-
> quate amounts to the hungry nations. The others like Argentina,
> Australia, Canada, and France charge the full commercial price.
> When a 10,000-ton freighter filled to the scuppers with free Food
> for Peace sails out of port a specific component of U.S. wealth is
> shipped out; wealth in the form of 200 tons of nitrogen, 41 tons of
> phosphorus, and 50 tons of potassium. Multiply these figures by the
> approximately 16,500 ten-thousand-ton freighter loads shipped out
> under this program and you will see that the portion of our soil's
> fertility thus lost forever is a significant part of our natural resources.
> We have every right to insist that this free food be used for the
> benefit of the United States. Until recently we were rushing to India
> alone 1,000,000 tons of grain a month, or three to four ships *each day*.

The Limits of Aid

New York Times editor James Reston stated some time ago that continued foreign aid with no population reduction effort would lead to reaction from the American people. As the Paddocks and others point out, the result of "aid" seems the opposite of aid, leading to more and more population, demanding more and more aid.

It is also true that there are those who seek profit from the situation. Some have fat-salaried jobs doling out assistance, some have businesses that stand to gain. The Paddocks mention four groups in this latter category: common carriers, farm machinery manufacturers, fertilizer manufacturers, and banks and other lenders. Surely statements like those of one manufacturer that it might be necessary to provide the developing-nation farmers with mechanized equipment almost at the hand-tool level, and headlines in a business weekly that "World Hunger Threatens U.S. Profits!" do little to ennoble the cause of world aid.

However, to claim that the interest of the developed nations in helping the less-privileged is simply selfishness or self-preservation is not to be fair or logical. If we feared war from the developing nations the safest course would be to leave them to their own devices, since increased hunger and starvation would weaken them further and make them far less of a threat. The efforts taken by the developed countries are largely humanitarian, and will continue to be so. It is this demonstrated fact of man's humanity to man that is the most optimistic harbinger of success in the global fight against hunger and other privation. It is this very real concern for the welfare of others that is likely to improve the lot of those who now have the least.

The United States has shipped billions of tons of food all over the world, dating back to the Hoover Plan following World War I and the Marshall Plan after World War II. Of a total of more than $100 billion in aid, about $15 billion has gone for food through P.L. 480, "Food for Freedom," and "Food for Peace." In 1966, when the United States was sending $254 million in food and $250 million in fertilizer to India, 25 other nations, including Canada, contributed a total of $70 million. A proposed new Food for Peace bill would obligate us with a commitment of $3.3 billion.

The Paddocks' point, however, is that despite our having done this and being willing to keep up our giving, everything is hopeless:

First of all, food shipments, continued year after year as in the present U.S. Food for Peace Program, seem to end up as a disservice to the recipient nations. Such shipments weaken their motivation to solve their own agricultural imbalance. Certainly that has been the case with India and probably Brazil.

An even clearer example is Egypt, to which the U.S.A. sent extraordinary amounts of food year after year. When the shipments eventually stopped, Russia sent the food needed. Egyptian agriculture remains in a hopelessly backward, primitive state. U.S. food contributed to this backwardness by taking pressure off Egypt's government—so that it did not have to face up to its country's agricultural problems.

Self-Help for the Hungry

Not surprisingly, few share the grimly brutal views of the Paddocks. In general the feeling is that here is a debt men owe their brothers—when people are hungry they must be fed, or at least helped to feed themselves. Yet almost 1,000 years ago, Maimonides said that truly the most commendable form of charity was one that would make charity unnecessary. Food for the hungry must eventually, in almost all cases, be grown on their own land. Fortunately they have land for that purpose, and providentially much of it is, or could be, more productive than that in our own country, as we have seen: it is hotter and receives more rainfall; heat and irrigation are vital to the production of food.

Malthus predicted worldwide famine 170 years ago, and he was not the first to consider such a food-population crunch. In the intervening years there have been catastrophic famines, although not of the kind he foresaw but tragedies of relatively short duration and limited to rather small areas, caused by bad weather or blight. Since Malthus, many others have cried the same warnings. Now a wave of neo-Malthusians have predicted black famine by 1970 (obviously a missed guess), by 1975, or fill in your own date. It is possible that such food crises may come about. There was widespread hunger in Southeast Asia several years ago after two years of bad weather and short crops. But Asia has surged back and more than matched population growth with food.

American farmers rallied to the so-called world food crisis some years ago and many of them lost money on surplus grain they couldn't sell for what it cost to produce. One farm authority has stated flatly that American food-producers could double their output in a decade if there was any reason to do so. With less than 1 percent population increase per year in this country, it will take us seven decades to double our population. If production can be brought up to our standards in the developing countries, they, too, should have no insurmountable problems, even with faster-growing populations.

It seems that this can be done, that increases in production can take care of increased population for some time yet. Hopefully, through continuing educational programs, increased communication, and advancing technology, the peoples of these lands will eventually get the message that it is no longer necessary to have ten or twelve children to guarantee ample hands and backs to till the soil in subsistence farming as they have historically and traditionally done.

The technology is available now to nourish everyone properly. FPC and other additives can provide proper protein intake at minimum cost. The remaining problems are mainly economic and administrative. Do we attempt to force-feed those who do not willingly eat what is set before them? Coercion is not only abhorrent to our way of thinking but perhaps a practical improbability.

Far better that we convince the undernourished through education, and perhaps better yet through an attractive diet it is to their benefit to partake of.

The "Indicative World Plan"—Strategy for Plenty

The United Nations is optimistic about the prospects of feeding the growing world. Its Food and Agriculture Organization, with the background of many years' work on the problem, has just issued what it calls "The Indicative World Plan for Agricultural Development," with the subtitle, "A Strategy for Plenty."

The sweeping yet realistic Indicative World Plan, or IWP, grew out of the first World Food Congress, held in Washington in 1963. The plan itself began in 1965, and was geared to cover the two decades through 1985, by which time there will be an estimated 1 billion more mouths to feed in Zone C, the "Third World," as it is called.

Authorized by FAO Director-General Addeke H. Boerma, the IWP wastes no time weeping and wailing but presents a straightforward plan intended to alleviate hunger in the developing countries. For this 44 percent of the world's people FAO spells out a program with five key objectives:

1. Securing the staple food supplies, with population growing at 2.5 to 3 percent per year. For most countries this means achieving a faster growth of cereal production.

2. Improving the quality of the diet. This calls for adjusting to the changes in the composition of the diet that accompany rising incomes and urbanization, and to the specific requirements in food policy which emerge from the analysis of the main dietary deficiencies. Here the supply of protein, particularly animal protein, is the crucial problem.

3. Earning and saving the foreign exchange that is crucial to financing overall development. Emphasis must be upon both boosting exports of agricultural products and reducing imports through economic substitution.

MORE MOUTHS WILL HAVE TO BE FED FROM SHRINKING LANDS

AVERAGE SIZE OF FARM FAMILY **6.4**

1962

EACH FARM FAMILY FED 2.7 PERSONS IN ADDITION TO ITSELF

2.9 HECTARES

1975

EACH FARM FAMILY WILL HAVE TO FEED 3.5 PERSONS IN ADDITION TO ITSELF

2.3 HECTARES

1985

EACH FARM FAMILY WILL HAVE TO FEED 4.1 PERSONS IN ADDITION TO ITSELF

2.0 HECTARES

ARABLE LAND PER FARM FAMILY

A graphic presentation of the problem facing the farmer and his customers. As population increases, there is less land available per person and more food must be produced per acre.
Food & Agriculture Organization

4. Providing a large part of the additional employment that will be needed over the period up to 1985, and at the same time helping to create opportunities for jobs in industries related to agriculture.

5. Increasing productivity through intensified use of the basic physical resources of land and water, including forests, oceans, and inland waters.

Increased production of cereal grains is the number-one priority. Backing it up is the increase of protein sources, particularly meat and meat products. To do this fastest, the IWP suggests the raising of more poultry and hogs, since they produce protein the fastest of the animals.

Hunger has been defined as the best measure of poverty. Ironically, poverty is also generally the best measure of hunger. Much of the problem stems from economics, and authority Max Millikan said that improved nutrition will not be possible without rising incomes in the developing countries. For a nation to exploit animal proteins purchased in the market, he estimated it would require incomes of $700 to $800 a year per capita. Two-thirds of the world's people have annual incomes less than $300. North American incomes are about thirty-eight times those of poorer Asia and Africa.

If the green revolution is to continue, and it must if the Third World is to be fed, another kind of green will be required, in the form of money. The price tag of IWP through 1985 is an estimated $110 billion. Continued help in the form of advice and loans must therefore come from the developed countries. But what better investment of time, goodwill, and money than to ensure food for all the world's peoples?

Dudley Kirk, an authority on food and population, stated in a speech at Miami University, Oxford, Ohio, in December 1968:

Far from facing imminent starvation the world has the best food outlook in a generation. So to the question, Are massive famines now inevitable? the answer is clearly No!

Hunger and malnutrition will still be with us. But in contrast with the views of the alarmists the facts are that, aside from war, famine has become rarer and rarer. Hunger is not new. *What is new is our awareness of it, our concern, and our expressed intention to do something about it.* . . .

The Ultimate Concern

For some time, then, it will not be necessary to halt population increase to stave off starvation, much as such a curb might help. There are, of course, other reasons why it might be wise to begin to check our increase with Zero Population Growth attained sometime in the near future.

The important consideration is not just total numbers of people or tons of food. The crux is optimum population for the "good life" we are forever seeking. There are at least two ways to reach this goal, which we must eventually achieve. One way—and the quicker—would be to set up a world dictatorship, aided by computers to monitor births and weed out the ill, the old, and the misfit—and perhaps those who subscribe to certain political beliefs along with them. The dictator might add a chemical to the environment so that there would be no births without the use of a neutralizing "conceptive." He would disperse the population in planned communities for all to have the *Lebensraum* so sought and prized. The dictator would tell us what was good for us and see to it that we got plenty of it. Then, presumably, we could love it or leave it.

One inhabitant would be too few for America. One billion would seem too many. There must be an optimum number somewhere between these two numbers that would assure the "good life" for Americans. That number obviously is not 1,000, or 1 million. These handfuls could not develop and use the resources of the nation sufficiently for the best life. Somewhere between a million and a billion, then. We are now at about 210 million, one-fifth of a billion. Should the brakes go on here? Or would 300 million be better able to utilize the blessings of nature?

Would it be possible to run the problem through a computer and arrive at the magic number? Probably not.

In 1900 there were some 189,000 people in what is now metropolitan Los Angeles. Not exactly elbow to elbow, and certainly nothing like the crowding now evident in the area with 7 million residents. But if population in Los Angeles had increased at the national average since 1900, how many people would live there today? The 7 million now rubbing elbows, half that number, or perhaps only 1 million? No, if the population of Los Angeles had increased at 1.2 percent annually since the turn of the century it would now number about 500,000 and rank almost as rural area. It is not so much population increase that is harming the environment as it is the urbanization that has taken place.

Peace Corps Volunteers at the Siniloan Rice Training Center learn how to grow the new strains of miracle rice in a two-week concentrated program.
Joan Larson

There is another way, probably the only way to prevent the Malthusian comeuppance that has lurked around the next corner for close to two centuries and cannot be ignored forever. This way will be achieved when the majority of us see and accept the facts of life and food and overcrowding. When we *voluntarily* set in motion a plan to match people to resources—to so number ourselves that we live not like rats in a cage or lemmings on the edge of a fjord, but as humans in a blessed environment made even more pleasant by man's culture and his technology. This is the slow way, the painful way, the way of many false starts and blind alleys. But it is surely the way to be preferred and it will be more lasting than any solution *forced* on us by a dictator, either human or electronic.

There is a wide and varied spectrum of the Great Population Explosion—from the view of alarmists who see no hope to that of laymen with yawning indifference. In between these extremes are the opinions of realists like Dudley Kirk. In their eyes no country is yet "down the drain" and must be sacrificed, but neither is everything rosy either. A great amount of dedicated—and costly—effort remains to be made by those with a deep and abiding concern for the enormous problems of population and food. While the battle is largely that of the undeveloped world, the hungry Third World, we in the more fortunate, developed portions must continue to help our brothers on two fronts—the control of population and the production of food. Somewhere in the middle is that happier world, "unvexed by war, untroubled by hunger...."

Bibliography

Appleman, Philip. *The Silent Explosion.* Boston: Beacon Press, 1965.

Bardach, John. *Harvest of the Sea.* New York: Harper & Row, 1968.

Bates, Marston. *The Prevalence of People.* New York: Charles Scribner's Sons, 1955.

Benarde, Melvin. *Race Against Famine.* Philadelphia: Macrae Smith Company, 1968.

Borgstrom, George. *The Hungry Planet.* New York: The Macmillan Company, 1965.

Brown, Lester. *Seeds of Change: The Green Revolution and Development in the 1970's.* New York: Frederick A. Praeger, Inc., 1970.

Carson, Rachel. *Silent Spring.* Boston: Houghton Mifflin Company, 1962.

Clark, Colin. *Population Growth and Land Use.* New York: St. Martin's Press, 1967.

Clark, Colin. *Starvation or Plenty?* New York: Taplinger Publishing Company, 1970.

Cook, Robert, and Lecht, Jane. *People.* New York: Population Reference Bureau, 1968.

Darwin, Charles Galton. *The Next Million Years.* New York: Doubleday & Company, 1952.

Dema, I. S. *Nutrition in Relation to Agricultural Production.* Rome, Italy: Food and Agriculture Organization of the United Nations, 1965.

Ettinger, Robert C. *The Prospect of Immortality.* New York: Macfadden-Bartell, 1969.

Fagley, Richard M. *The Population Explosion and Christian Responsibility*. New York: Oxford University Press, 1960.

Food and Agriculture Organization of the United Nations. *Agriculture in the World Economy*. Rome, Italy, 1963.

Food and Agriculture Organization of the United Nations. *Fisheries in the Food Economy*. Rome, Italy, 1968.

Food and Agriculture Organization of the United Nations. *A Strategy for Plenty: The Indicative World Plan for Agricultural Development*. Rome, Italy, 1970.

Freedman, Ronald, ed. *Population: The Vital Revolution*. New York: Doubleday & Company, 1965.

Hardin, Clifford, ed. *Overcoming World Hunger*. Englewood Cliffs, N.J.: Prentice-Hall, Inc., 1969.

Hauser, Philip. *Population and World Politics*. New York: The Free Press of Glencoe, 1958.

Hulse, Frederick S. *The Human Species*. New York: Random House, 1963.

Malthus, Thomas R. *Essay on the Principle of Population*. London: J. M. Dent & Sons, Ltd., 1816.

Millikan, Max, and Hapgood, David. *No Easy Harvest: The Dilemma of Agriculture in Underdeveloped Countries*. Boston: Little, Brown and Company, 1967.

Ng, Larry K. Y., and Mudd, Stuart, eds. *The Population Crisis: Implications and Plans for Action*. Bloomington: Indiana University Press, 1965.

Organski, A. F. K., and Organski, Katherine. *Population and World Power*. New York: Alfred A. Knopf, 1961.

Osborn, Fairfield, ed. *Population; the Vital Revolution*. New York: Doubleday & Company, 1962.

Osborn, Frederick. *On Population: Three Essays*. Princeton: Princeton University Press, 1958.

Ovington, J. D., ed. *The Better Use of the World's Fauna for Food*. Symposia of the Institute of Biology. London, 1963.

Paddock, William, and Paddock, Paul. *Famine—1975!* Boston: Little, Brown and Company, 1968.

President's Science Advisory Committee. *The World Food Problem: Report of the Panel on the World Food Supply*. Washington, D.C.: Government Printing Office, 1967.

Rock, John. *The Time Has Come*. New York: Alfred A. Knopf, 1963.

Sanger, Margaret. *My Fight for Birth Control*. New York: Farrar & Rinehart, 1935.

Sax, Karl. *Standing Room Only: The World's Exploding Population*. Boston: Beacon Press, 1955.

Shepard, Paul, and McKinley, Daniel, eds. *The Subversive Science*. Boston: Houghton-Mifflin Company, 1969.

Smith, David T., ed. *Abortion and the Law*. Cleveland: The Press of Western Reserve University, 1967.

U.S. Department of Agriculture. *Food for Us All: The Yearbook of Agriculture*. Washington, D.C.: Government Printing Office, 1969.

U.S. Department of Agriculture. *Protecting Our Food: The Yearbook of Agriculture*. Washington, D.C.: Government Printing Office, 1966.

Whitten, Jamie. *That We May Live*. New York: Van Nostrand–Reinhold Company, 1966.

Index

Bellamy, W. Dexler, 240
Beria, Lavrenti, 53–54
Besant, Annie, 35
Beukels, William, 188
birth control and contraception,
 34–60, 67, 247, 248–49
 antinatalists, 42–47, 76–78
 and Communism, 53–54
 by compulsory methods, 9, 38, 43–
  47 *passim*, 77, 259, 260
 and desire to procreate, 47
 developed countries, 24, 40
 developing countries, aid to, 9,
  49–50, 52–53, 55–56, 58, 248–49
 homosexuality proposed, 9, 46
 political factors, 53–54, 57
 primitive cultures, 34, 38
 pronatalists, 47–49, 50, 57
 religious beliefs, customs, and su-
  perstitions, 36–37, 47, 50, 54,
  56–57
 sexual gender, influence on, 48
 tax compensations for small families proposed, 9, 46
 tax penalties for large families proposed, 9, 43, 46, 248
birth control and contraception,
 methods of, 37–39
 abortion, 9, 25, 35, 38–39, 42, 43,
  45–46, 53, 54, 59, 248, 249
 castration, 38
 chastity, 37
 coitus interruptus, 37
 condom, 37, 42, 249
 intrauterine device (IUD; loop),
  9, 38, 42, 49, 50, 58, 59, 247–48,
  249
 jelly, 42
 pill, 37, 38, 42, 43, 44, 58, 59
 rhythm method, 36–37, 42
 sterilization, 9, 38, 39, 42, 43, 45,
  46, 58, 59, 248, 249
Birth Control League, 35
birthrate, 24–25, 26, 31, 32
 fertility, 22–26 *passim*
 reproduction rate in a generation,
  23
Bishop, Marcus, 240
Blake, Judith, 44
Blatnik, John A., 63
Boerma, Addeke H., 256

Borgstrom, George, 3, 11, 150, 151,
 168–69, 176, 179, 184–85, 235–
 36
Boswell, James, 24, 142
Bradlaugh, Charles, 35
Brazil: agricultural production, 203,
 219, 254
 land, arable, 200
 livestock, 162
Breder, D. M., Jr., 84
Brown, Lester, 11, 212–13, 214, 215
Brush Foundation: birth control, aid,
 50
Bulgaria: birth control, abortion, 39
Bulletin of the Atomic Scientists, 8,
 224, 244
Burbank, Luther, 139

California: agricultural production,
 127, 128
calories and kilocalories, 89–91, 103–
 04, 105
 and body size, 116
 need per day, 111, 112
Cambodia, 189
Cameroons, 115
Canada: agricultural production, 141,
 197, 218, 252
 protein consumption, 160
cannibalism, 221
carbohydrates, 11, 12, 91, 92–93, 98,
 103, 104–05, 107, 110, 140, 143,
 241, 246
 vs. proteins, 11, 12, 101, 106, 154–
  56, 176
CARE: birth control, aid, 50
Carleton, Mark Alfred, 139
Carrel, Alexis, 237
Castro, Josue de, 39–40
cellulose: experiments with use as
 feed, 240
Central America: agricultural production, 140–41
 nutrition and body size, 116
 polycarencil infantile, 115
 see also Latin America
cereal grain, see grain
Ceylon: agricultural production, 213
 death rate, 29
Chalkhill, John, 173